TRAILS
& Treats

A HIKER AND RUNNER'S GUIDE TO GREAT TRAILS AND GOOD EATS IN NORTH CAROLINA

Palmer McIntyre & Hollis Oberlies

PURPLE ZANTE PRESS
GREENSBORO, NC

Dedicated to new and seasoned trail enthusiasts who appreciate a sweet or savory treat after a day outdoors. May you be inspired by each and every chapter of this book.

And to the good folks in our Great Trails State who preserve and maintain the natural spaces, and to those who own and operate local establishments. Your work makes all the difference.

Table of Contents

FOREWORD 1

INTRODUCTION 3

ABOUT THIS GUIDE 4

PLANNING YOUR DAY OUT 6

STATE MAP WITH TRAIL LOCATOR 10

TRAIL CHECKLIST 11

TRAIL FEATURES CHART 12

TRAILS (listed by region)

MOUNTAIN REGION

1 Art Loeb Trail at Black Balsam Knob and Tennent Mountain 14

2 Crabtree Falls 19

3 Table Rock Mountain and the Chimneys, Linville Gorge 24

4 Appalachian Trail at Roan Mountain 30

5 Profile Trail, Grandfather Mountain State Park 35

6 Rough Ridge and Tanawha Trail 40

7 Green Knob Trail at Sims Pond 45

8 Summit Trail, Elk Knob State Park 50

TRIAD REGION

9 Stone Mountain Loop Trail, Stone Mountain State Park 56

10 Salem Lake Trail 61

11 Uwharrie Trail at Little Long Mountain 66

12 Laurel Bluff Trail 71

13 Downtown Greenway, Greensboro 76

14 Guilford County Farm 82

15 Cane Creek Mountains Natural Area 87

TRIANGLE REGION

16 Crow Branch Overlook Trail, Carolina North Forest 93

17 Johnston Mill Nature Preserve 98

18 Occoneechee Speedway Trail 103

19 Cox Mountain Trail, Eno River State Park 108

20 Little River Regional Park and Natural Area 114

21 Company Mill Trail, William B. Umstead State Park 119

22 Ann and Jim Goodnight Museum Park, NC Museum of Art 124

23 Bailey and Sarah Williamson Preserve 129

CHARLOTTE REGION

24 Fall Mountain Trail, Morrow Mountain State Park 135
25 McAlpine Creek Park and Greenway 140
26 Charlotte Rail Trail 145
27 Latta Nature Preserve 150
28 Duke Kimbrell Trail, Seven Oaks Preserve 156
29 Pinnacle Trail, Crowders Mountain State Park 161
30 Bakers Mountain Park 166

TRAIL RACES 172

ACKNOWLEDGMENTS 174

CREDITS 175

ABOUT THE AUTHORS 176

RECIPES TO KEEP YOU GOIN'

Uncle Spike's Pancakes 29
Caroline's Granola 55
Palmer's Trail Cookies 81
GORP 92
Good Morning Muffins 113
Kristen's Energy Bites 134
Sunrise Egg Cups 155

Life is short.
Take the trip.
Hike the trail.
Eat the cake.

Foreword

My idea of being at home in North Carolina has always been outside, and often on a trail. As a kid, my Scout troop hiked the Appalachian, and at summer camp (shout out to the Foxhole, the oldest boys' Kanuga cabin, circa 1989) we hiked the trails in and around Henderson County so often we came to know them as our own. When I moved to Greensboro in 1997, the first time I felt at home might have been on any of the rental front porches in College Hill, but it might also have been out on the trail systems that trace the lakes north of town. All of us grad students had dogs in those days, and we used to cut the dogs loose out there to chase deer and fight geese and get pretty lost and then found again. I could not say the word "lake" to that grad school dog unless I meant it, unless I really was going to take her.

These days I'm a little smarter and a somewhat better citizen and my dogs are leashed up when I'm on the trail, but I've got two boys who like to scramble and clamber around, who like to climb boulders and cross creeks and seek out something special, something new, when we're done. We once made cucumber sandwiches after one of those grad-school expeditions; something about a proper hike required a proper bite to eat, even then. Anymore, I love to find a brewpub and steal a late-afternoon pint after I've chased our beasts a few miles, plus sometimes a well-earned basket of fries.

I would have loved to find this book back in my grad-school days, and I'm delighted to find it now. It'll live in the back of the van with the first-aid kit and the emergency matches: I'm often in some little town with a few hours to kill and kids and dogs who need a good walk and a good snack. Or maybe it'll live inside, actually, on the kitchen table—an answer waiting for anyone in our house who's wondering what we're going to do with our day. "Here," I'll say, passing it along. "Find us somewhere good, and let's go."

> — *Drew Perry*
> Author of *Kids These Days* and *This Is Just Exactly Like You*

Introduction

Trails of all kinds, whether tucked into the edge of the woods in a neighborhood park, up steep mountain summits, or circling a quiet, secluded pond, provide an escape from the everyday and connect us to the beauty of the natural world. A little fresh air and exercise in a serene setting can be the perfect respite from our busy lives and a way to refresh our minds.

Trails can be enjoyed in many ways, but our favorite is to explore by foot, either hiking or running, taking the time to fully absorb our enchanting and peaceful surroundings. Although runners and hikers explore trails at different paces, both relish in the beauty of the landscape, and both need to refuel their bodies after a day of adventure and exploration in nature.

While there are a number of North Carolina trail guides available, *Trails & Treats* is different. It combines our passion for the outdoors and good food by offering a collection of exceptional trails alongside a curated selection of delicious local eats for pre- or post-trail hunger and thirst. This unique, first-time guide, written by a female hiker and runner duo, is designed for both seasoned hikers and trail runners, as well as first-time explorers. It offers 30 different trails and more than 70 treats, plus additional options for trail extensions and area highlights.

We hope these pages will inspire you to step out of your daily and weekly routines, to create your own adventures, and to discover the varied and beautiful landscapes of North Carolina. You don't have to travel far to find great places to hike or run and explore incredibly diverse natural spaces. There are often trails close to your home or within a short drive that will bring you joy and gratitude, along with a good workout. Venturing to nearby towns and cities close to these trails can be easy day trips and truly feel like a vacation. Allow time to explore local establishments and meet the people who make our state great. The people are one of North Carolina's best attributes.

This guide is not for the coffee table, but meant to become a favorite companion, tucked into the side compartment of your car door, your backpack, or placed on your bedside table after a day on the trails, reminding you to plan your next day out. Write in the margins about what you saw. Jot down the dates you explored certain trails. Note what you ordered at a restaurant, or what other treats you discovered in a particular town after your time on the trails. Tuck in photos from your adventures, or fold the corners of the pages on favorite chapters you want to revisit during a different season. Record the memories of your special experiences. Perhaps you saw a flock of wild turkeys race across a field or saw the setting sun from a most magnificent view atop the mountain. Maybe you noticed tadpoles swimming circles in the shallows at the edge of a pond. Note when you had the pleasure of a certain friend or family member who joined in your adventure. Use this guide for more than its own words.

As you turn the pages of *Trails & Treats*, imagine the world of discovery waiting for you. Invite a friend and give these trails a try. Each path is an opportunity to explore, create memories, and renew your inner spirit. We can't wait to hear about your North Carolina adventures.

— Palmer and Hollis

About This Guide

We have selected trails in four general areas of the state—the mountains, the Triad, the Triangle, and the Charlotte area—and have organized the book in a clockwise fashion. The trails highlighted represent some of our favorites but are just a sampling. With more than 1,000 trails to choose from in North Carolina, it was challenging to narrow our list down to 30. We intentionally chose trails that offer different types of experiences, showcase diverse regional landscapes, range in popularity, and are managed by a variety of agencies and organizations.

Many of the featured trails also include other interesting attributes, such as historical and/or geological significance, rare flora, a scenic vista, special water features, or are in a unique cultural or urban setting. A chart highlighting features of each trail can help you decide the right one for your desired experience each time you plan a getaway. Check off the list of trails as you try them.

There is a chapter for each of the 30 trails that includes length of trail, level of difficulty, where to find the trailhead, extra information about the area, trail running thoughts, and ideas to extend your day. You will see suggestions for surrounding connector trails, picnic spots, and other not-to-miss stops on your way to or from the trail. There are a variety of trail length options to choose from, and many hikes can be extended or shortened depending on your interest. Also included are trail tips to help you plan a fun and safe day.

If you are sticking to hiking, this guide will provide recommendations for you to try solo or together with family or friends. If you are a hiker or road runner and have always wanted to try trail running, this book can be that bit of inspiration. If you are a trail runner, these pages provide workout options specific to each trail.

In each chapter, we recommend different types of treats to give you choices depending on your cravings and preferences. These are some of our favorite places that are close to the selected trails, locally owned, source local ingredients, are reasonably priced, welcome sweaty bodies, and are kid- and often pet-friendly. All of them are great for a meal or a snack before or after your adventure, with savory and/or sweet options. Featured are cafés, restaurants, breweries, bakeries, delis, markets, general stores, pizzerias, pubs, diners, coffee shops, ice cream parlors, and even an outpost. We know businesses can unexpectedly change ownership, operating hours, or even close their doors, so double-check online for the most up-to-date information before going. Like the trails, there are many others to consider, but we hope our treat suggestions will give you a head start to finding just the right one to fit your day.

Because we want to make sure our bodies are properly fueled before and during our hikes and runs, we have included some of our favorite breakfast and trail snack recipes. Interspersed between chapters, these easy-to-make recipes provide tasty and nourishing treats to keep you feeling strong throughout your day on the trail. They are all tried and true, and inspired by good friends and family who love healthy food.

There are endless possibilities of exploration within *Trails & Treats*. Remember, it's not always about the destination, or the goal, but the little moments along the way. So get started, and dream up your next day out!

A journey of a thousand miles
begins with a single step.

— Lao Tzu

Planning Your Day Out

Whether you are planning a short hike or run or a longer day hike, there are a few essentials to properly prepare for your trail adventure. You don't need fancy gear to have a great day out on a trail, but there are some important items to consider. As you plan, know that the most important thing is to be prepared for the weather. The next most important thing is to take water, snacks, and a first aid kit for accidents. We recommend not carrying too much weight—only take what you need.

Always let someone know your plans and make sure your cell phone is fully charged before you go (and turn off Wi-Fi to save your battery). You may find one of the many trail apps helpful, such as AllTrails, Trailforks, or Strava. Because there may not be cell service where you are, download or take a picture of the trail map so you can find your way. Or pack this guide with you!

Here's our list of trail essentials:

Clothing: Layers are important, keeping you warm in the cool mornings, but easily removed as you warm up. Chance of rain? Toss a waterproof jacket or poncho into your backpack. Understand that the weather in the mountains can change quickly and unexpectedly, so always have extra layers and rain gear on hand in that region. A beanie helps keep you warm in cool weather, and a brimmed hat will protect you in sunny areas (along with sunscreen and a long-sleeve shirt).

Water: Too much is better than not enough, but water is also heavy, so try to gauge what you will need to stay properly hydrated. A general recommendation is about one half-liter of water per hour of moderate activity. You can carry your water in bottles or a hydration vest/pack. Never drink water from streams without treating it.

Footwear: One of the most important things is comfortable shoes. You don't need new hiking boots or running shoes to tackle the trails, but choose something sturdy and supportive, and wear socks that prevent blisters.

Backpack: We like to carry a small backpack that can hold water, snacks, a first aid kit, and any extra layers. Choose one with a waist belt and your shoulders will be much happier!

Trail snacks: Snacks will keep your energy up and save you and anyone with you, especially little ones, from getting hangry! Emergency chocolate or another treat is always handy with young kids to help them reach the end. Always take a little more than you think you need since hiking burns calories quickly, and your trail may take longer than expected.

*Hollis' favorite
trail running gear*

▲

*Palmer's hiking gear
suggestions* ▶

Sun protection: Include in your pack sunscreen, sunglasses, a long-sleeve shirt, and a brimmed hat for open areas.

Basic first aid supplies: Pack adhesive bandages, an elastic wrap bandage, and antihistamine at a minimum.

Hiking poles or sticks: These can save your knees going uphill and downhill.

Insect repellent: Depending on where you are hiking and the time of year, insect repellent may be important. You especially want to stay safe from mosquitoes and ticks.

A few things to watch out for:

Weather: Check the forecast in advance and take the appropriate clothing and outer layers needed to be comfortable and dry.

Poisonous plants: You will find poison ivy, poison oak, and poison sumac throughout North Carolina. Contact with any of these plants will cause an itchy rash. Remember: "leaves of three, let it be."

Ticks: Ticks can cause some very unpleasant diseases, including Rocky Mountain spotted fever and Lyme disease. The best deterrents are insect repellent containing DEET or clothing treated with permethrin. Remember to check your body when you return home.

Bees: If you see a concentration of bees during warmer months, it could indicate a nest in the ground or a tree. Move away quickly! Carry an over-the-counter antihistamine in your first aid kit in case of an allergic reaction to a sting.

Snakes: Most of the snakes you might encounter on a trail are harmless, but there are a few venomous species found across the state, including copperheads and timber rattlesnakes. These are uncommon, but do keep an eye out on the path. The best thing to do if you see a snake is not to disturb it and keep your distance. If bitten, seek medical assistance.

Minimizing Environmental Impact

We all love a pristine experience in the woods. As more people discover North Carolina trails, there is inevitably negative impact due to erosion caused by heavy foot traffic and trash, including pet waste. Respecting the rules of the places we visit and sticking to the trail will help preserve our outdoor spaces for others and future generations. Outdoor NC Leave No Trace Principles (©Leave No Trace) provide guidance to reduce our collective effect on our fragile natural areas:

Plan and prepare: Choose lesser-known areas and avoid times of high use.

Stick to trails: Minimize erosion and protect trailside plants. If muddy, walk through it instead of widening the path to avoid it.

Trash your trash: Pack out what you take in, including food scraps, cigarette butts, pet waste, and other litter, some of which takes years to decompose and are unhealthy for wildlife.

Leave it as you find it: Rock stacking in and beside streams disrupts natural habitats for aquatic species. Snap a picture instead of collecting rocks, flowers, etc. so you leave them for others to enjoy. Don't leave your mark by carving into trees.

Keep wildlife wild: Observe creatures from a distance and especially refrain from feeding wild animals.

Be considerate of others: Be respectful of others on the trail and let nature be your music. When passing others, let them know with a friendly voice. (Hikers/runners going uphill have the right of way.)

Hiking/Trail Running with Dogs

Many dogs love an outdoor adventure, especially on a trail! Follow rules and regulations, keep your dog on a leash, and clean up after your dog so others can experience an unspoiled environment. Make sure to pack treats and enough water for your pet.

Hiking with Kids

Kids naturally love exploring, and trails are a wonderful way to inspire a love of the outdoors from a young age. Select a hike that is easier, be flexible, and let your little ones set the pace. Hikes with water features are always a hit, especially where water is safely accessible for wading and exploring. Be sure to pack sufficient snacks. Sometimes kids need a little extra to keep going when they are hot and tired. To avoid meltdown moments, take breaks and have some sweet treats handy to keep energy levels up. (Consider making and packing a treat from one of our recipes!) Give your family plenty of time to find the unexpected—a flower to study, an interesting tree, or a glimpse of an animal in the wild. The hikes in this guide are very appropriate for children.

Selecting a Trail

All 30 trails can be enjoyed by novice or experienced hikers/runners of all ages, and range in length and difficulty. When selecting a trail, consider your fitness level (as well as the people you are with), your desired level of challenge, and the distance/driving time to get to the trailhead. Use the chart on page 12 to review trail features that might inspire your selection. Are you looking for a destination with a water feature? Maybe it's a loop trail that you desire? Perhaps you want to visit something historical? Or are you seeking an incredible vista? This chart can help steer you to something just right to fit your day.

As you plan, don't try to go too far or too fast too soon. If you are new to hiking or trail running, build your endurance by beginning with shorter and flatter options and work your way up to longer and steeper trails. If you are new to trail running, it may take time to get used to running on uneven surfaces. At any level of experience, using a journal can be inspirational to track your fitness over the weeks, months, and years. Record mileage or the number of hours you spend hiking or running in nature, and which trails you hiked or ran. Seeing your progress can give you a great sense of accomplishment. Use the check list on page 11 to note the trails you explore.

Never the Same Twice

Whether planning for the first or hundredth trek, it's important to remember that no trail is the same twice. Consider visiting the same space multiple times. There are many ways to explore a trail: at different times of the day, in multiple seasons, traveling the opposite direction, at varied speeds, and solo or in the company of others. You are guaranteed to have a unique experience every time. Try a meet-up with local hiking and running clubs. Members in these groups are always interesting people to talk with about their experiences and can get you started or provide new ideas to try. Visit your nearest outdoor or running store or look online for a group. We wish you safe, invigorating, and inspiring days on the trails!

BOONE
ELKIN
WINSTON-SALEM
GREENSBORO
DURHAM
RALEIGH
CHAPEL HILL
MORGANTON
HICKORY
ASHEVILLE
ASHEBORO
CHARLOTTE
30

North Carolina Trail Adventures

MOUNTAIN REGION

- ❑ 1 Art Loeb Trail at Black Balsam Knob and Tennent Mountain
- ❑ 2 Crabtree Falls
- ❑ 3 Table Rock Mountain and the Chimneys, Linville Gorge
- ❑ 4 Appalachian Trail at Roan Mountain
- ❑ 5 Profile Trail, Grandfather Mountain State Park
- ❑ 6 Rough Ridge and Tanawha Trail
- ❑ 7 Green Knob Trail at Sims Pond
- ❑ 8 Summit Trail, Elk Knob State Park

TRIAD REGION

- ❑ 9 Stone Mountain Loop Trail, Stone Mountain State Park
- ❑ 10 Salem Lake Trail
- ❑ 11 Uwharrie Trail at Little Long Mountain
- ❑ 12 Laurel Bluff Trail
- ❑ 13 Downtown Greenway, Greensboro
- ❑ 14 Guilford County Farm
- ❑ 15 Cane Creek Mountains Natural Area

TRIANGLE REGION

- ❑ 16 Crow Branch Overlook Trail, Carolina North Forest
- ❑ 17 Johnston Mill Nature Preserve
- ❑ 18 Occoneechee Speedway Trail
- ❑ 19 Cox Mountain Trail, Eno River State Park
- ❑ 20 Little River Regional Park and Natural Area
- ❑ 21 Company Mill Trail, William B. Umstead State Park
- ❑ 22 Ann and Jim Goodnight Museum Park, NC Museum of Art
- ❑ 23 Bailey and Sarah Williamson Preserve

CHARLOTTE REGION

- ❑ 24 Fall Mountain Trail, Morrow Mountain State Park
- ❑ 25 McAlpine Creek Park and Greenway
- ❑ 26 Charlotte Rail Trail
- ❑ 27 Latta Nature Preserve
- ❑ 28 Duke Kimbrell Trail, Seven Oaks Preserve
- ❑ 29 Pinnacle Trail, Crowders Mountain State Park
- ❑ 30 Bakers Mountain Park

Trail Features

		TRAIL SURFACE	VISTAS/OVERLOOK
MOUNTAIN REGION			
1	Art Loeb Trail	NATURAL	•
2	Crabtree Falls	NATURAL	•
3	Table Rock Mountain and the Chimneys, Linville Gorge	NATURAL	•
4	Appalachian Trail at Roan Mountain	NATURAL	•
5	Profile Trail, Grandfather Mountain State Park	NATURAL	•
6	Rough Ridge and Tanawha Trail	NATURAL	•
7	Green Knob Trail at Sims Pond	NATURAL	•
8	Summit Trail, Elk Knob State Park	NATURAL	•
TRIAD REGION			
9	Stone Mountain Loop Trail	NATURAL	•
10	Salem Lake Trail	NATURAL	•
11	Uwharrie Trail at Little Long Mountain	NATURAL	•
12	Laurel Bluff Trail	NATURAL	•
13	Downtown Greenway, Greensboro	PAVED	
14	Guilford County Farm	NATURAL	•
15	Cane Creek Mountains Natural Area	NATURAL	•
TRIANGLE REGION			
16	Crow Branch Overlook Trail, Carolina North Forest	NATURAL	•
17	Johnston Mill Nature Preserve	NATURAL	
18	Occoneechee Speedway Trail	NATURAL	
19	Cox Mountain Trail, Eno River State Park	NATURAL	•
20	Little River Regional Park and Natural Area	NATURAL	•
21	Company Mill Trail, William B. Umstead Park	NATURAL	•
22	Ann and Jim Goodnight Museum Park	BOTH	•
23	Bailey and Sarah Williamson Preserve	NATURAL	•
CHARLOTTE REGION			
24	Fall Mountain Trail, Morrow Mountain State Park	NATURAL	•
25	McAlpine Creek Park and Greenway	BOTH	
26	Charlotte Rail Trail	PAVED	
27	Latta Nature Preserve	NATURAL	•
28	Duke Kimbrell Trail, Seven Oaks Preserve	NATURAL	•
29	Pinnacle Trail, Crowders Mountain State Park	NATURAL	•
30	Bakers Mountain Park	NATURAL	•

WATER FEATURE	HISTORIC SITE OR ART TRAIL	HIKE FORMAT	DIFFICULTY LEVEL	PARK TYPE/ LAND MANAGEMENT
		LOLLIPOP	MODERATE	US FOREST SERVICE
•		LOOP	MODERATE	NATIONAL PARK SERVICE
		OUT & BACK	MODERATE	US FOREST SERVICE
		OUT & BACK	MODERATE	US FOREST SERVICE
•		OUT & BACK	STRENUOUS	NC STATE PARKS
•		OUT & BACK	MODERATE	NATIONAL PARK SERVICE
•		LOOP	MODERATE	NATIONAL PARK SERVICE
		OUT & BACK	STRENUOUS	NC STATE PARKS
•	•	LOOP	STRENUOUS	NC STATE PARKS
•		LOOP	EASY	CITY OF WINSTON-SALEM
•		OUT & BACK	MODERATE	US FOREST SERVICE
•		OUT & BACK	MODERATE	CITY OF GREENSBORO
	•	LOOP	EASY	CITY OF GREENSBORO
•	•	LOLLIPOP	EASY	GUILFORD COUNTY
•		LOOPS	MODERATE	ALAMANCE COUNTY
•		LOOP	EASY	UNC-CHAPEL HILL
•	•	LOOPS	EASY	TRIANGLE LAND CONSERVANCY
•	•	LOLLIPOP	EASY	NC STATE PARKS
•	•	LOLLIPOP	MODERATE	NC STATE PARKS
•		LOOPS	MODERATE	DURHAM & ORANGE COUNTIES
•	•	LOLLIPOP	MODERATE	NC STATE PARKS
•	•	LOOPS	EASY	NC NATURAL & CULTURAL RESOURCES
•		LOOPS	EASY	TRIANGLE LAND CONSERVANCY
•	•	LOOP	MODERATE	NC STATE PARKS
•	•	MULTIPLE	EASY	MECKLENBURG COUNTY
	•	OUT & BACK	EASY	CITY OF CHARLOTTE
•	•	LOLLIPOP	MODERATE	MECKLENBURG COUNTY
•		OUT & BACK	EASY	CATAWBA LANDS CONSERVANCY
•		LOOP	MODERATE	NC STATE PARKS
•		LOOP	MODERATE	CATAWBA COUNTY

Art Loeb Trail at Black Balsam Knob and Tennent Mountain

Distance: **5 miles, lollipop loop**
Difficulty Level: **moderate**
Trailhead: **Blue Ridge Parkway, Milepost 420.2**

The climb speaks to our character, but the view, I think, to our souls.
— Lori Lansens

This area of the Blue Ridge Parkway is especially scenic and ruggedly beautiful, and this section of the Art Loeb Trail is no exception. The trail is legendary and absolutely worth a visit for the incredible 360-degree long-range views from these highest peaks of the Great Balsam Mountains. This moderately challenging 5-mile loop begins in a fragrant balsam fir forest, then opens up to a brushy meadow to continue the steady climb up to Black Balsam Knob

(0.7 miles, elevation 6,214 feet). A plaque on a wide, gray rock outcrop near the summit commemorates Art Loeb, the trail's namesake. The trail then rolls across the sunny, grassy ridgeline to Tennent Mountain. There are numerous picnic/snack spots on top of either peak, but you will find fewer people on Tennent Mountain (1.9 miles, elevation 6,040 feet).

Once you descend from the top of Tennent Mountain, take a left to follow the Ivestor Gap Trail, which is more like a rocky dirt road. Just before the Ivestor Gap parking area, turn left onto the Art Loeb Spur Trail, following a short but steep climb back up toward Black Balsam Knob. At the top, turn right to follow the Art Loeb Trail back to the parking area. This area is very popular, so come early or later in the day (think sunrises and sunsets) or pick a weekday. Good shoes, a hat, and sunscreen are a must for this sunny, rocky trail. Note that trail signage is limited in wilderness areas.

More to Know

The 30-mile Art Loeb Trail is the longest and most challenging trail in Pisgah National Forest, connecting the Davidson River Campground near Brevard with the Daniel Boone Boy Scout Camp in Haywood County. It gains more than 9,000 feet of elevation one way, and 7,000 feet of elevation if hiked in the other direction, truly meaning it's "uphill both ways." The trail, dedicated in 1969, honors Arthur J. Loeb, a trailblazer who pioneered the idea of a long-distance trail in Pisgah National Forest, and who is remembered as an "industrialist, conservationist, and hiker who deeply loved these mountains." It remains one of the most popular long-distance hikes in Pisgah. North of Tennent Mountain the trail passes by Shining Rock, named for the large, white quartzite rock outcropping near its summit, and Cold Mountain, made famous by the novel and film. These peaks are bald due to extensive logging and a series of wildfires over time.

Running Thoughts

The hilly nature of Art Loeb is a good challenge. As a reminder, the earlier you get on the trail, the better. This single-track trail gets very busy on weekends, and you may find it hard to run the trail at a continuous pace, forcing you to slow down in populated areas to pass hikers. You will want to stop every so often to take in the stellar surrounding views and get a selfie atop the mountain. Also, make sure to bring plenty of water, since the sun exposure will be significant.

Getting There

There are two places to park to access the Art Loeb Trail in this area. If you are heading south on the Blue Ridge Parkway, just past Milepost 420, look for Black Balsam Knob Road (Forest Service Road 816) on the right. The parking area for the Art Loeb Trail is along the road at about 0.8 miles. If this parking area is full, an alternative is to continue for another 0.5 miles to the Ivestor Gap Trailhead parking area. If you park here, you can access Black Balsam Knob via the Art Loeb Spur trail. It's a bit steeper and climbs more overall, but it's also a nice hike and useful if the first parking area is full. Turn left at the top to reach the summit of Black Balsam Knob.

Extend Your Trip

An alternative to Black Balsam Knob (or in addition to) is the hike to Sam Knob. You can do this as an out and back (2.5-mile round trip) or as a 3.9-mile loop that includes the stunning summit of Sam Knob (elevation 6,045 feet) and the Flat Laurel Creek Trail. Follow the Sam Knob Trail from the Ivestor Gap Trailhead parking area through a grassy meadow and take the spur trail through laurel thickets to the summit. Go back the way you came, or if you want to do the full loop, return to the Sam Knob Trail and turn left on the Flat Laurel Creek Trail to return to the parking area. There are several creek crossings and small scenic cascades on the Flat Laurel Creek Trail. The trail can be wet in areas, so be sure to wear appropriate footwear.

Since the Art Loeb Trail is a long-distance trail, you can easily extend your trip to a longer day trip to reach Shining Rock (10-mile round trip) and/or Cold Mountain (18-mile round trip), or a backpacking trip, as a point-to-point or a loop. These sections of the Art Loeb Trail are in the Shining Rock Wilderness Area, where trails are generally not signed or blazed. There

Trail Tip: *Layer your clothing. Throughout the day it may be necessary to shed or add layers due to weather changes, elevation gains, sunny or shady parts of trails, and your body's natural tendency to heat up during exercise. Carry a small pack and be prepared to make adjustments as you hike or run.*

N
W E
S
Little East Fork Pigeon River
Fork Mountain Trail
Ivestor Gap Trail
Art Loeb Trail
Tennent Mountain 6040 ft.
Graveyard Ridge Trail
Ivestor Gap Trail
Art Loeb Trail
Sam Knob 6045 ft.
Mountains-to-Sea Trail
Black Balsam Knob 6214 ft.
Sam Knob Trail
P
Flat Laurel Creek Trail
Flat Laurel Creek
P
Upper Falls Trail
Art Loeb Trail
Yellowstone Prong
Black Balsam Knob Rd
Blue Ridge Parkway
0   0.25   0.5
Miles
Featured Trails:
Art Loeb Trail/ Ivestor Gap Trail
Other Trails
Roads
Rivers, Creeks, & Lakes
Public & Protected Lands

is frequently no cell phone service, and bear canisters are required if camping overnight. Be sure to do your research if planning a longer hike than the featured loop trail.

Graveyard Fields, a popular hiking area, is only 2 miles north on the Blue Ridge Parkway (Milepost 418.8), and it features two spectacular waterfalls on the Yellowstone Prong. Bonus: the parking lot has restrooms.

Hungry? Let's Eat!

Brevard, the closest town and about a 45-minute drive from the trail, is quaint, has good vibes, and is full of delicious food options for the outdoor adventurer. If you decide to get takeout, there are public outdoor tables in town where you can enjoy your treat or meal.

Bracken Mountain Bakery
42 S. Broad St., Brevard, NC 28712

Specializing in European-style breads and pastries as well as some regional American favorites, Bracken Mountain Bakery is going to brighten your day! This bakery offers some of the best cookies, supplying that extra energy to get you up the trail with a smile. The bakery items are all delicious and made from scratch every morning with wholesome, organic ingredients. It's hard to pick just one given the vast selection of muffins, scones, croissants, danishes, sweet rolls, turnovers, cookies, and breads. Need a coffee fix? A full coffeehouse drink list is available. Their coffee beans are roasted in town, specifically for them by The Brown Bean Coffee Roasters. In 2022, Bracken Mountain Bakery was #7 out of the 20 best bakeries of the South in *Southern Living* magazine. A can't miss when in Brevard. Note that they are closed on Sunday and Monday.

Cup & Saucer / Mercantile / Brevard Pizza Works
36 E. Main St. A, Brevard, NC 28712

Cup & Saucer has been serving locals and visitors alike since 2019. The talented baristas and bakers are ready to serve specialty coffee drinks, house-made baked goods, breakfast, and lunch. Don't miss the fresh biscuits, made daily. Coffee is roasted by Cooperative Coffee Roasters in Asheville. The Cup & Saucer Mercantile, located just steps down the public alleyway, showcases products from local farmers and makers and offers customers a sitting space to cozy up with their beverages or desserts. Interested in pizza? Specializing in Roman crust and Detroit-style crispy pan pizza, Brevard Pizza Works is a great choice. Online orders only. This is a collaboration project with Cup & Saucer, with pickup in the Mercantile. Plans for their own pizza parlor are "in the works." These two businesses are closed on Sunday. Check hours online.

Crabtree Falls

Distance: **3.1 miles, loop**
Difficulty Level: **moderate**
Trailhead: **Blue Ridge Parkway, Milepost 339**

Choose only one master—nature.
— Rembrandt

This scenic trail takes you to the spectacular Crabtree Falls, where Big Crabtree Creek cascades over a 70-foot rock cliff to form one of the tallest waterfalls along the Blue Ridge Parkway. We recommend following the loop in a counterclockwise direction. The trail starts in the parking lot by Crabtree Falls Campground, passing the amphitheater, then crossing the campground road. Beyond the road, the trail starts to descend steeply through a beautiful hardwood forest and rhododendron thickets with several sets of stairs. At the bottom, you will find an enchanting boulder field covered with mosses, ferns, and wildflowers right before you reach the magnificent falls.

Find a quiet spot to enjoy the impressive view. Spray from the waterfall can cool you off on a hot summer's day, but beware that wet rocks are slippery. The climb back up starts out with some steep switchbacks with dramatic views of the falls from the top, then becomes much more gradual, following Big Crabtree Creek, where you will find a smaller set of falls before ending up back at the campground.

More to Know

This area of the Blue Ridge Parkway was named for the many crabapple trees that once grew here, but before the Blue Ridge Parkway was constructed, the falls were known as Murphy's Falls. There was a small community established here during the heyday of logging, including cabins, a grist mill, a woodworking shop, a blacksmith shop, a Baptist church/schoolhouse, and a store. The surrounding meadows and open space reflect the farming history of this area.

Running Thoughts

One approach to this trail is to run the flats and hike the hills. This method will give you a good workout without wearing you out on the steeper hills and switchbacks, especially climbing back up after viewing the falls. Take this at a gentle pace, so you have time to notice the magical landscape leading up to the falls and can manage some technical footwork over rocks and roots. Build in time to stop at the waterfall and get a few selfies and some reflection time during your "water break."

Trail Tip: *One of the most important items for hiking or running trails is footwear. Look for a shoe/boot that offers excellent support, make sure you have plenty of wiggle room for your toes, and ensure a snug fit around the ball of your foot and heel. Most outdoor outfitters carry both trail running and hiking footwear. Try on shoes with the socks you plan to wear to get an accurate fit. Lace up snugly to prevent movement and blisters. Waterproofing your shoes/boots will provide additional protection.*

Getting There

The parking area for Crabtree Falls is at Milepost 339 on the Blue Ridge Parkway at the Crabtree Falls Campground, 5 miles south of Little Switzerland and 15 miles north of Mount Mitchell. A portable toilet is on-site.

Extend Your Trip

An interesting place to explore western North Carolina's mining history is the nearby Museum of North Carolina Minerals, located just off the Blue Ridge Parkway near Little Switzerland (Milepost 331 at the junction with NC Hwy. 226). Our ancient Blue Ridge Mountains contain some of the richest deposits of gems and minerals in the world, and this museum showcases more than 300 varieties, including spectacular emeralds, rubies, amethyst, and quartz. The interactive displays explain the geological processes that formed our rich mineral deposits and describe how they have been mined, processed, and used to create all kinds of products. There is also a gift shop with souvenirs and books. The museum is free and open every day from April to the end of October, but closes for lunch. Each September, the museum hosts a reenactor encampment to commemorate the journey of Revolutionary War fighters called the Overmountain Men on their way to the Battle of Kings Mountain, a battle recognized as one of the turning points in the Southern Campaign of the Revolutionary War.

If you are taking NC Hwy. 80 back down to Marion, and you feel like making a quick stop for ice cream and a little fishing, pull into Buck Creek Trout Farm (8385 Buck Creek Rd.). You are 100% guaranteed to catch fresh trout, which they will clean for you to take home in exchange for a small tip.

N
W E
S
Crabtree Falls
Big Crabtree Creek
Crabtree Falls Campground
Amphitheater
Blue Ridge Parkway
0
0.25
0.5
Miles
Featured Trail:
Crabtree Falls Loop Trail
Other Trails
Roads
Rivers, Creeks, & Lakes
Public & Protected Lands

Hungry? Let's Eat!

Switzerland Cafe and General Store
9440 NC Hwy. 226A, Little Switzerland, NC 28749

Switzerland Cafe has been serving some of the best hickory-smoked pork for over 30 years, landing them an honored spot on the North Carolina Barbecue Trail. They have one of the largest wood-fired smokehouses in the state. A favorite of many diners is the applewood-smoked trout. Also offered are sandwiches, salads, soups, and quiche. Save room for a homemade dessert, with choices such as carrot cake, strawberry rhubarb pie, and Kentucky bourbon pecan pie. The welcoming staff, great service, and menu favorites make Switzerland Cafe a not-to-miss mountain destination. The adjoining general store sells T-shirts, gift items, and their own rib and 'que sauces. They are open seasonally, from March through November. Check online for exact dates, which are weather dependent.

Famous Louise's Rock House Restaurant
23175 Linville Falls Hwy., Linville Falls, NC 28647

At The Rock House, you can say you have eaten in three counties in one stop! On the National Register of Historic Places and located at the tripoint where McDowell, Avery, and Burke Counties meet, this family-owned restaurant serves up comfort food that will satisfy both kids and adults. It's the sort of place that might conjure up some kid memories of your own. Tempting menu items include mountain trout, catfish, barbecue, pot roast, and meatloaf, and a selection of country sides to accompany your order. Plenty of burgers

and sandwiches are also offered. Or maybe you are stopping by for breakfast before the trail? They open early and are fixin' hotcakes, omelets, biscuits, breakfast sandwiches, and your fill of coffee. Serving standard American fare with a friendly atmosphere, this is a true mountain staple. Don't miss the pie. Note they are open Wednesday through Saturday.

Table Rock Mountain and the Chimneys, Linville Gorge

Distance: **Table Rock, 2 miles, round trip, out and back; the Chimneys, 2 or more miles, round trip, out and back**
Difficulty Level: **moderate**
Trailhead: **map to Table Rock Mountain Parking Area**

Look deep into nature, and then you will understand everything better.
— Albert Einstein

Known as the Grand Canyon of the East, the rugged Linville Gorge Wilderness Area should be on the bucket list of all North Carolina hikers. With its jagged peaks, chimney-like rocky outcroppings, and steep cliffs formed by erosion resistant quartzite, it is magnificent in all seasons. Table Rock Mountain and the Chimneys are a favorite destination in the Gorge to experience its impressive beauty. Table Rock Mountain's distinctive, 3,950-foot summit is visible from many areas of western North Carolina and was a sacred place for the Cherokee people, who called it "Attocoa."

This chapter highlights two short, out-and-back trails, both which extend from the parking area: one to Table Rock Summit and the other to the Chimneys. Both sections are part of the NC Mountains-to-Sea Trail and Pisgah National Forest. The Table Rock Trail departs from the parking lot by the kiosk and begins with a steep climb up. After reaching the top, make your way past a stone foundation from a bygone building and carefully scramble over the rough, rocky outcroppings to enjoy stunning, 360-degree views of the Gorge with the Linville River below; Hawksbill Mountain, Grandfather, and the Roan Mountain balds to the north; the Chimneys, Shortoff Mountain, and Lake James to the south; and rolling green hills to the east. Take the spur trail to Devil's Cellar for another overlook and fascinating rock formations.

The Chimneys Trail leaves from the opposite side of the parking lot next to the pit restrooms. After a short climb up, the trail opens to a series of dramatic rock formations along a narrow ridge on the canyon rim with spectacular views around every corner. Kids will love this hike, with so many interesting rocks, but keep a close watch, as there are numerous sheer cliff drop offs. Along the way, you may spot rock climbers and cross paths with backpackers. Since it's an out and back, follow the trail for as long as you like before turning around. The Chimneys end about a mile out, but the trail continues to Shortoff Mountain, 5.6 miles from the picnic area/parking lot.

More to Know

The Gorge is 12 miles long, carved by the Linville River as it descends a dramatic 2,000-foot drop to the Piedmont between two parallel ridges. In a few places, the Gorge is almost 2,800 feet deep from the ridges to the riverbed. Settlement and logging were impractical in Linville Gorge because of the rugged terrain, so the Gorge has one of the few remaining populations of old growth forest in the Blue Ridge Mountains.

Running Thoughts

If you like the challenge of scrambling rocky ledges and are an experienced trail runner, give Table Rock or the Chimneys a try. However, if you prefer to run something a little less strenuous, then head to Lake James State Park. There are many miles and multiple trails, some of which are minutes from

Trail Tip: *Know that on certain trails you may not have cell service, especially in the mountains. Take a photo or screen capture of the trail map on your phone so you can easily access it while hiking. Of course, make sure your phone is sufficiently charged before hitting the trail, and turn off your Wi-Fi to save your battery!*

Fonta Flora Brewery (highlighted in the treats portion of this chapter). These single track trails offer gently rolling, shaded terrain, with views of the water along many sections. Try the 3.6-mile Mills Creek Trail from the Paddy's Creek Access. Connect it with other trails in the park to extend your mileage, if desired. A run here, paired with a hike at Table Rock and the Chimneys, makes for a spectacular day or weekend excursion.

Getting There

Getting to Table Rock Mountain is half the adventure! There are two options, and both involve a long but scenic drive on a narrow and bumpy gravel road. From NC Hwy. 181, take Gingercake Road, then stay left onto Table Rock Road and follow for 7 miles. You will pass trailheads for Sitting Bear, Hawksbill, and Spencer Ridge. Alternatively, from NC Hwy. 181, but much closer to Morganton, take a left onto Simpson Creek Avenue, then a quick right onto the gravel Table Rock Road for 12 miles to reach the parking area. The trailhead, which has pit restrooms and a shaded picnic area, is open from April to December. Parking is limited, so arrive early or during off times. There are some campsites near the parking area for an easy car camping. No water source exists at the trailhead.

Extend Your Trip

There are dozens of hikes in Linville Gorge, most of which are strenuous. It is easy to combine a trip to Table Rock Mountain with nearby Hawksbill Mountain. Don't miss the Linville Falls Trail (Blue Ridge Parkway Milepost 316.5) which passes through remnants of a virgin hemlock forest and has spectacular views of the falls. Shortoff Mountain is also beautiful (13 miles, round trip, from NC 126, if closer access at Wolf Pit Road is closed). The popular overlooks at Wiseman's View and other trails are accessible from the gravel Old NC Hwy. 105. In addition to numerous trails, the Paddy's Creek Access at Lake James State Park offers a pristine beach for swimming as well as paddleboard, canoe, and kayak rentals. There are a variety of camping options within the park: drive-in, walk-in, and boat-in sites.

Mountains-to-Sea Trail
Little Table Rock Trail
Linville Gorge Trail
Linville River
Table Rock Mountain 3931 ft.
Table Rock Mountain Rd
P
The Chimneys 3521 ft.
Mountains-to-Sea Trail
N
W
E
S
0   0.25   0.5
Miles
Featured Trails:
Table Rock Summit Trail
The Chimneys
Other Trails
Roads
Rivers, Creeks, & Lakes
Public & Protected Lands

Hungry? Let's Eat!

We recommend a visit to Morganton, with its vibrant downtown and many spots to relax and curb your hunger after a day's adventure. The historic Courthouse Square has benches and greenspace for a picnic, if you want to continue your day outdoors.

Food Matters Market and Cafe
210 Avery Ave., Morganton, NC 28655

For grab-and-go items, consider the stop "Where People and Food Matter." This community grocery has a café with many options of smoothies, sandwiches, salads, and soups, all made with local, fresh, organic ingredients. The market supports local producers and sells foods from the region. Café tables are available at the market, or order take-out and head over to the Courthouse Square. Food Matters Market and Cafe has a sister location in Brevard, for future trail (and treat) adventures over that way.

Moondog Pizza
304 S. Sterling St., Unit 200, Morganton, NC 28655

At the entrance, climb one long flight of stairs, where you'll be greeted by Moondog's friendly staff, ready to seat you at a table in their bright, open dining space with light hardwood floors and brightly colored chairs, or you can grab a seat at the bar in the back of the restaurant. Moondog serves up delicious pizzas, salads, sandwiches, wraps, strombolis, and calzones every day but Monday. Try one of their signature pizzas (Burk-n-Stock, The Dogfather, or Spicy Chix), or build your own from more than 40 toppings. Gluten-free, dairy-free, and vegan options are also available. Orders come on tin plates, and the tables have rolls of paper towels to use as napkins. Say no more.

Fonta Flora Brewery Whippoorwill Farm
6751 NC 126, Nebo, NC, 28761

Located on 9 acres of pastureland, this farmhouse brewery is a true treat and a perfect end to your outdoor day. Let the kids play while the adults relax on the vast lawn or patio of the barn brewhouse. Dogs are welcome, too, on leash. Find a table or bring a picnic blanket, and order something delicious from the food trucks on-site. In the tasting room, Fonta Flora's knowledgeable staff can help you find just the right beer for the moment. They recognize craft beer as an artistic endeavor, and their commitment and connection to good people who supply locally sourced ingredients makes their beers stand out. Consider taking home your favorites as packaged products from their cooler, as a souvenir of sorts, reminding you of your great trail day. The farm taproom is closed on Monday and Tuesday. The original taproom in Morganton is open 7 days a week. Run Club at the Pub meets on Monday nights.

UNCLE SPIKE'S PANCAKES

Uncle Spike's pancakes are a hearty breakfast treat before a day's adventure! Make it your own by topping with fruit and nuts, or add berries or chocolate chips into your batter. If you like breakfast for dinner, this is a delicious meal after a day on the trails.

DRY INGREDIENTS:

1 cup white flour
¼ cup masa flour
¼ cup whole wheat flour
¼ cup flax meal
¼ cup rolled grains of your choice
   (oats, rye, barley, wheat)
1 tablespoon turbinado sugar
2 teaspoons baking powder
½ teaspoon baking soda
½ teaspoon sea salt

WET INGREDIENTS:

1 egg
1½–1¾ cups buttermilk
1 tablespoon vegetable oil

DIRECTIONS:

In a large bowl, combine the dry ingredients. Then add the wet ingredients into the dry, and stir together. Heat a skillet with a dab of vegetable oil and a pat of butter over medium heat. Once the oil/butter combo is hot, swirl to coat the pan. Add ½ cup of batter to the skillet. Flip when nicely browned. When both sides are golden, top with maple syrup or honey, and any combination of yogurt, berries or any fruit, nuts, or chocolate chips.

Appalachian Trail at Roan Mountain

Distance: **4.3 miles, round trip, out and back**
Difficulty Level: **moderate**
Trailhead: **Carvers Gap (NC Hwy. 261/TN Rt. 143)**

The pull of the mountain is like gravity for my soul.
— Heather Day Gilbert

S panning five mountain summits, the Roan Mountain Highlands never disappoint in any season with their expansive and stunning 360-degree views. With the largest expanse of mountain balds in the Appalachians all above 4,000 feet in elevation, the Highlands have something to offer in all four seasons—wildflowers all summer, especially the spectacular Catawba rhododendron in June; wild blueberries that ripen in August; glorious fall colors; and magical frost and snow in the winter. This hike follows the well-known Appalachian Trail (AT) across three high-elevation grassy balds descending slightly into gaps in between each.

From Carvers Gap, follow the AT's white blazes north through the wooden stile on the east side of the road (across the road from the parking lot). After a short climb through a fragrant and enchanting balsam fir forest, the trail opens up to Round Bald at 0.6 miles, followed by Jane Bald with its large rock slabs. Then, after another short and steep climb through tunnels of dense rhododendron, you will arrive at your destination: Grassy Ridge Bald at 6,184 feet high, 2.15 miles from the trailhead. There is a trail intersection at 1.8 miles where the AT veers off to the left. Be sure to follow the blue side spur trail to reach the summit of Grassy Ridge Bald. On clear days look for the profiles of Grandfather Mountain and Mount Mitchell.

Take plenty of water, a windbreaker/raincoat, and a hat and sunscreen, as the weather can be windy and change rapidly, and shade is limited on the sunny balds. The parking lot gets full on the weekends, so we recommend you arrive early to find a spot, or choose a weekday.

More to Know

With their wide open vistas, the Roan Mountain Highlands are one of the most iconic stretches of the AT, the famous 2,190-mile-long footpath extending from Georgia to Maine. This special area is one of the most biologically diverse in the world, with many specialized habitats, including high-elevation rock outcrops, southern Appalachian bogs, grassy balds, rich spruce-fir forests, and the world's largest natural rhododendron garden. There are more federally listed plant species here than in the Great Smoky Mountains National Park.

Running Thoughts

We can't say it enough: the weather is dynamic in the mountains. Based on this fact alone, it's a good idea to wear a small running pack at Roan Mountain so that you can carry a few essentials: plenty of water (a backpack with a bladder is helpful), a snack, your phone/camera to capture the

stunning views, sunscreen to reapply as needed, and a light windbreaker or rain jacket for changes in the weather. Extend your mileage as desired using the AT.

Getting There

Carvers Gap is on the North Carolina/Tennessee border, where NC Hwy. 261 and TN Rt. 143 meet. There is a parking lot with restrooms at the gap.

Extend Your Trip

Continue on the AT northbound from the Grassy Ridge Bald spur trail for an additional up-and-down 3.7 miles to reach the former location of the storied Overmountain Shelter at Yellow Mountain Gap. The Overmountain Shelter was a famous historic red barn and was the largest and one of the most unique shelters on the AT. From the spur trail intersection, the trail summits Yellow Mountain at 2.8 miles, then descends through Deep Gap, passing the Stan Murray Shelter at 3 miles before reaching the open area where the Overmountain Shelter once stood. Tent camping is allowed in the open area. The hike to Yellow Mountain Gap from Carvers Gap is 11 miles, round trip.

For a completely contrasting experience, follow the AT south for a 3.2-mile round trip to Roan High Knob through a lush and mossy fir forest. Roan High Knob is the highest-elevation shelter on the entire AT at 6,285 feet of elevation. It is surrounded by spruce and Fraser fir trees, similar to a Canadian forest. You can veer off the AT to visit the Roan High Knob overlook, catching exceptional views near the former site of the historic Cloudland Hotel, a popular Roan Mountain destination in the late 19th century. You won't get the views like you do on the open side of the trail, but the forest is magical.

Trail Tip: Some hikes are really sunny, so wear a hat, bring along sunscreen to protect your skin from sunburn and ultraviolet (UV) radiation, and don't forget sunglasses to shield your eyes. If possible, aim to hike on shaded trails between 10 a.m. and 4 p.m. when the sun shines strong, and use mornings for open-area hikes. Reapply sunscreen every two hours or more frequently on hot, sweaty days.

N
W E
S
TN 143
Tennessee
Carvers Gap
Round Bald
5826 ft.
Jane Bald
5807 ft.
Appalachian Trail
Appalachian Trail
Roan High
Knob
6285 ft.
SR 1348
North
Carolina
Grassy
Ridge
Bald
6184 ft.
NC 261
Charles Creek
Salt Creek
Little Rock Creek
0   0.5   1
Miles
Featured Trail:
Appalachian Trail
at Roan Mountain
Other Trails
Roads
Rivers, Creeks, & Lakes
State Boundary
Public & Protected Lands

Hungry? Let's Eat!

Banner Elk is a quaint mountain town just 26 miles from the trail, tucked in between two ski resorts and popular trail destinations, and home to Lees-McRae College. Many restaurants and pubs are open year-round to curb your hunger and give you a place to relax after your trail experience. Have fun exploring the town!

Banner Elk Cafe & Tavern
324 Shawneehaw Ave. S. Hwy. 184, Banner Elk, NC 28604

Banner Elk Cafe & Tavern has a warm lodge feel, and their welcoming staff will take good care of you no matter where you sit: indoors in the comfortable dining room, at the central bar, or on the patio in the shade of umbrellas, surrounded by lovely, well-tended plantings. The café and lodge each have their own menu and own kitchen, which gives you a plethora of meal options. Even the pickiest eater will find a favorite! Breakfast is served daily from 7 to 11 a.m. There are loads of good choices, with eggs, omelets, breakfast sandwiches, and items from the griddle. Lunch and dinner menu options are even more extensive, ranging from appetizers, subs, sandwiches, wraps, burgers, pizzas, salads, Italian pastas, seafood entrées, and more. The bar serves specialty cocktails, or you can enjoy a beverage from their decently long beer and wine list. Come for live music on Friday and Saturday nights, join trivia night on Tuesday, or play music bingo on Wednesday nights—all provide a great way to wind down after a good day on the trails.

BE Scooped Ice Cream Shop
144 Azalea Cir. S.E., Banner Elk, NC 28604

Opened in 2019, BE Scooped is sweet-as-can-be, located in the heart of town, on the backside of The Village Shops. This family-owned ice cream shop serves 16 flavors, all delicious choices, hand scooped with a smile. Choose a cup, cone, or waffle cone, and the size of the scoop. Flavors rotate, with current ones listed on their website. Or maybe you would rather have a creamy milkshake? They've got you covered. And don't forget a treat for your furry, four-legged friend. Made fresh in-store, the "Dog Ice Cream," consisting of Greek yogurt, bananas, and peanut butter, is a sure hit. We love that BE Scooped travels with an ice cream truck and is involved in local school and special community events. At certain times of the year (as posted online), look for the golden ice cream scoops hidden in the town park. If you find one, return it to BE Scooped for a free scoop of ice cream!

Profile Trail, Grandfather Mountain State Park

Distance: 7.2 miles, round trip, out and back
Difficulty Level: strenuous
Trailhead: 4198 NC Hwy. 105 N., Banner Elk, NC 28604

I am at home among trees.
— J.R.R. Tolkien

The Profile Trail at Grandfather Mountain is one of North Carolina's iconic trails and a must do for adventure seekers and those looking for a challenge with a big payoff. This extremely well-maintained, but steep, trail climbs the western face of Grandfather Mountain, from NC Hwy. 105 to the summit ridge, with 1,775 feet of elevation gain. The trail starts out over relatively easy terrain for the first 0.5 miles, crosses scenic tributary streams to the Watauga River, then begins to climb. There are a number of well-placed stone steps and rocky outcroppings and bluffs, including the famous Grandfather profile view for which the trail is named at mile 2.8, before finally reaching the crest of Grandfather Mountain.

The Profile Trail ends at the intersection with the Grandfather Trail where you turn left through a magical spruce-fir forest to reach Calloway Peak. Calloway Peak is the highest point on Grandfather Mountain at 5,946 feet, with open spots and stunning views in all directions. There are several big, sturdy ladders to help climb over some of the steeper rock outcroppings. For this reason, taking pets on this hike is not recommended.

Prepare well for this hike, as weather on Grandfather Mountain can change abruptly. Be sure to take plenty of water. There is a piped spring near the top, but do not drink untreated water. Pack layers, as the temperature can be significantly cooler at the top.

More to Know

The Profile Trail traverses a number of distinct ecological zones, starting in a hardwood forest thick with wildflowers and rhododendron; rising through a northern hardwood forest with more red spruce; then reaching a cool and damp boulder field forest dominated by yellow birches, mosses, and ferns; and finally entering a unique and beautiful Canadian fir forest at the summit. Grandfather Mountain is widely recognized as the most ecologically significant mountain in the Eastern United States, with 70 species of rare, threatened, and endangered plants and animals.

Grandfather Mountain became a state park in 2009 with the purchase of 2,456 acres from the Morton family, who owned the entire mountain. The family still owns and operates the private attraction with paid entry on Grandfather Mountain, which includes the famous Mile High Swinging Bridge.

Trail Tip: A brisk hiking pace is 3 mph, and an average pace is 2 mph, but steep hills will slow you down. For every 1,000 feet of elevation, add around an hour to your hiking trip. For trail runners, expect a slower pace than your road pace.

Running Thoughts

The Profile Trail is a challenging, long run with many scenic views. Be sure to bring plenty of water, some trail cookies and apple slices, or another source of energy to refuel at the top. On your return, when you most likely will notice tired legs, be conscious of picking up your knees and feet to help you stay upright! Or run up, enjoy the incredible views, and then hike back down. Either way, you are in for a great workout.

Getting There

The parking lot for the Profile Trail is located on NC Hwy. 105 in between Boone and Linville. From Linville, travel 4.3 miles north. From Boone, travel 12.6 miles south. The entrance to the parking lot is on the south side of the road. Follow the entrance road about 0.25 miles to the large parking area for the Profile Trail. There is a new State Park building with restrooms, a covered patio area, water, and a boot-washing station at the start of the trail.

Extend Your Trip

Those seeking a much longer adventure can turn right at the intersection of the Profile Trail and the Grandfather Trail toward MacRae and Attic Window Peaks, for a 2.5-mile (one-way) extension to the famous Mile High Swinging Bridge. There are bigger ladders along this rugged stretch of trail. Another, longer way to access Calloway Peak is to take the Daniel Boone Scout Trail from the Boone Fork parking area on the Blue Ridge Parkway (Milepost 299.5), for a 7-mile loop hike that includes the Cragway Trail and part of the Nuwati Trail.

Hungry? Let's Eat!

The Pedalin' Pig BBQ
4235 NC Hwy. 105, Banner Elk, NC 28604

What's their secret? Maybe it's the slow-roasted, locally sourced meats, use of hickory-smoked hardwoods, the seasonal ingredients from the region, or the homemade sauces and rubs. The Pedalin' Pig "combines gourmet ingredients with a splash of High Country style," serving customers mouthwatering barbecue with delicious Southern side dishes. Wash it down with sweet tea,

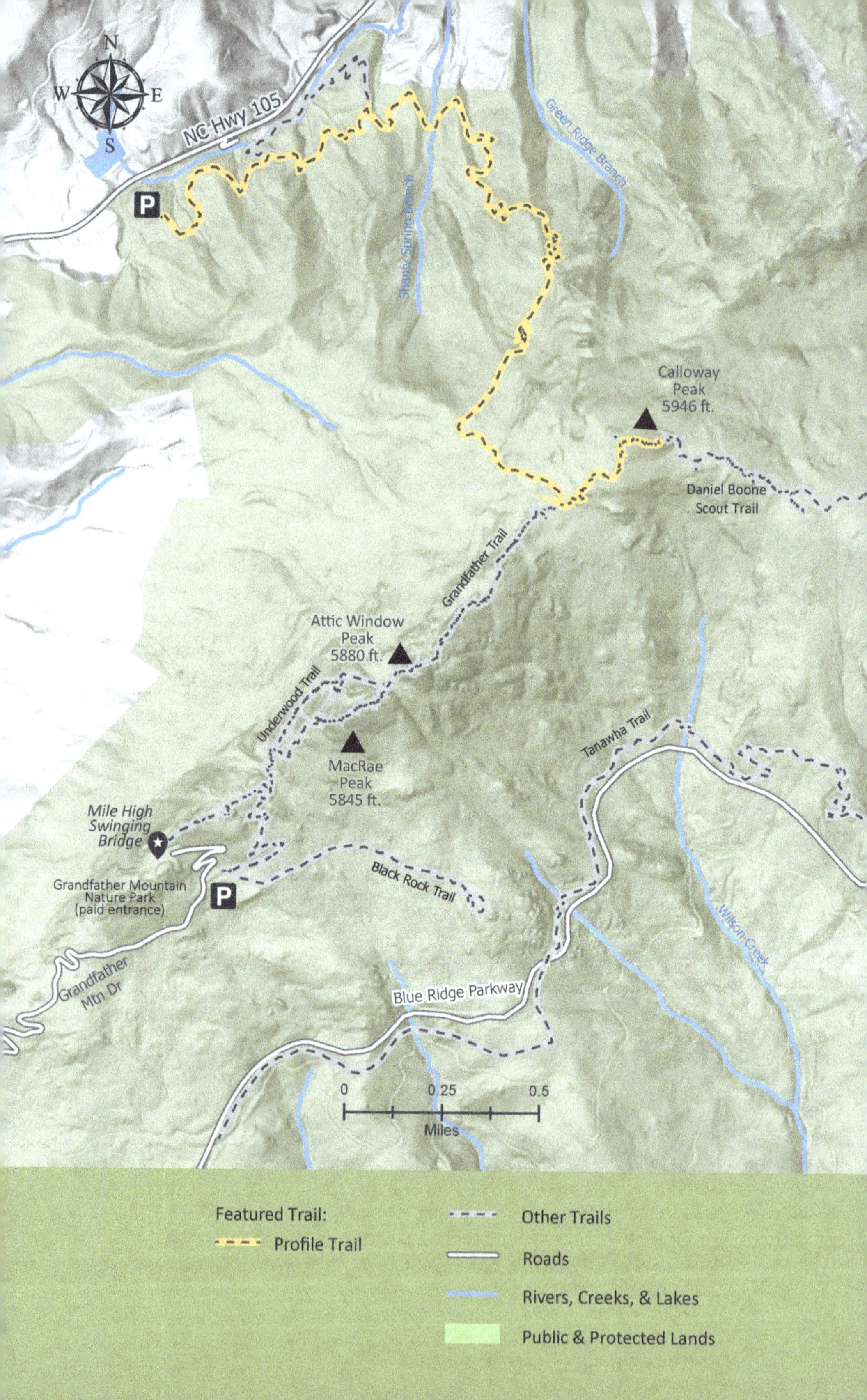

N
W E
S
NC Hwy 105
P
Shanty Spring Branch
Green Ridge Branch
Calloway Peak 5946 ft.
Daniel Boone Scout Trail
Grandfather Trail
Attic Window Peak 5880 ft.
Underwood Trail
MacRae Peak 5845 ft.
Tanawha Trail
Mile High Swinging Bridge
Grandfather Mountain Nature Park (paid entrance)
P
Black Rock Trail
Wilson Creek
Grandfather Mtn Dr
Blue Ridge Parkway
0   0.25   0.5
Miles
Featured Trail:
Profile Trail
Other Trails
Roads
Rivers, Creeks, & Lakes
Public & Protected Lands

a draft beer, or local cider. Don't forget to leave room for banana pudding! There are plenty of booths and tables in their dining room for you and your family or your hiking buddies. Vegetarian and gluten-free options are available on the menu. The Pedalin' Pig is open every day for lunch and dinner. If in Boone, check out their sister location, also on NC Hwy. 105.

Grandfather Vineyard & Winery
225 Vineyard Ln., Banner Elk, NC 28604

Grandfather Vineyard & Winery is a small, family-owned business right in the heart of the High Country. It is located on the Watauga River just off NC Hwy. 105, between the Profile Trail parking lot and Boone. Relax on their outdoor patio with a lovely view of the vineyard and surrounding landscape. Head into the tasting room and sample a flight of their wines. Pair it with local cheeses and crackers, charcuterie, or other snacks. Try wines by the glass or order a bottle to share at the table. Kids are quite welcome, as are furry friends (on leash). For those under 21, they offer other beverage options such as muscadine grape juice, apple cider, sodas, and mocktails. Live music in the vineyard is frequent, so check schedules online and kick back or cut a rug with some local, live entertainment. Open year-round, but closed on Tuesday during the winter.

Mast General Store
630 W. King St., Boone, NC 28607

Mast General Store is a classic family- and employee-owned mercantile offering a unique experience. With two main entrances and two different sides to the store (connected inside), there is truly something for everyone. There are men's and women's outdoor clothing, shoes, outerwear, and gear on one side of the store, and gift items, foods, candy, games, and toys on the

other. This side of the store was originally a separate business started in 1988 called The Candy Barrel, officially becoming part of Mast General Store in 1997. The famous barrels adorned with red checkered cloth contain assorted candies sold by the pound. Many of the candies stocked are traditional brands and flavors. It's fun to pick and choose from among old favorites and try new ones. You can also find a section devoted to Moon Pies in many flavors. Open 7 days a week, the Boone store is one of 11 locations across the state and South. The original location in Valle Crucis is housed in a historic 1883 building, also serving as the town post office, with its very own zip code. Stop in and visit the other Mast General Store locations as you travel the state. They are all historically unique!

Rough Ridge and Tanawha Trail

Distance: 2 miles, round trip to Rough Ridge, out and back (extend on Tanawha Trail for more miles)
Difficulty Level: **moderate**
Trailhead: **Blue Ridge Parkway, Milepost 302.8**

Hiking is not escapism; it's realism. The people who choose to spend time outdoors are not running away from anything; we are returning to where we belong.

—Jennifer Pharr Davis

Rough Ridge is one of North Carolina's most famous hikes along the Blue Ridge Parkway, leading to spectacular views of Grandfather Mountain, the Linn Cove Viaduct, and Linville Gorge. This short hike begins at the north end of the parking lot, first crossing a scenic stream cascading down the mountain. The trail becomes steep, leading to a series of stairs and board-walks traversing fragile rocky outcroppings above the treeline, and eventually the Rough Ridge summit at 4,773 feet in elevation. There are some benches and a number of stone overlooks along the way, perfect for resting and taking in the incredible views. Rough Ridge is especially known for sunsets and brilliant fall colors.

Signs along the way provide information about the sensitive natural environment and species on this rugged peak. Please respect instructions to stay on the trail and explore the stone overlooks at designated places. The parking lot can get full during peak times, so plan for an early or late start on weekends or choose a weekday to visit. The total elevation climb from the parking area is 480 feet.

More to Know

Rough Ridge is part of the 13.5-mile Tanawha Trail that follows the Blue Ridge Parkway, extending from Julian Price Park (Milepost 297) to Beacon Heights (Milepost 305.2). The Tanawha Trail is part of the NC Mountains-to-Sea Trail. Tanawha is the Cherokee word for "fabulous hawk or eagle," an appropriate name for this trail that offers hikers spectacular views of distant mountains. The trail was completed in 1993 and winds through a wide diversity of ecosystems, including mountain laurel and rhododendron thickets, hardwood coves, spruce and fir forests, boulder fields and cascading streams. Tanawha was also the original name for Grandfather Mountain, whose rugged peaks create a profile of a grandfather's face which can be seen from great distances.

The Linn Cove Viaduct, visible from Rough Ridge, is a 1,243-foot concrete bridge. It was completed in 1987 at a cost of $10 million and was the last section of the Blue Ridge Parkway to be finished. The Viaduct is considered an engineering marvel that was designed to minimize impact on the sensitive ecology of Grandfather Mountain. The bridge was built from the top down; 153 precast bridge segments weighing 50 tons each were lowered into place by crane with no heavy equipment on the ground.

Running Thoughts

First, hike to see the views atop Rough Ridge. Begin your run by continuing on the Tanawha Trail heading south toward Beacon Heights, or turn around and head north toward Julian Price Park. It's a great trail for a long run if you are prepared with water and snacks. Run it out and back, turning where needed to get in your desired mileage, then back down to the parking area. Or after enjoying views from Rough Ridge, drive to the nearby Bass Lake Loop Trail on the outskirts of Blowing Rock. This peaceful, wide, flat trail is ideal for mile repeats around the 1-mile loop. On summer mornings, you might see cross country teams training at Bass Lake.

Getting There

The Rough Ridge Trail starts from the right-hand side of a parking lot located at Milepost 302.8 on the Blue Ridge Parkway. After climbing a few stairs from the parking lot, you will reach an intersection with the Tanawha Trail. Turn left to follow the sign toward Linn Cove and Beacon Heights. There are no restrooms in the parking area.

Extend Your Trip

If you want a bit of a longer hike from the Rough Ridge parking lot, you can follow the Tanawha Trail past the Rough Ridge summit toward the Linn Cove Visitor Center (approximately 5 miles, round trip). If it is open, you can also park at the Linn Cove Viaduct Visitor Center at Milepost 304.4 to hike the short distance leading under the viaduct.

An option for a much more ambitious hike or run is to complete the entire 13.5-mile Tanawha Trail one way by leaving a vehicle at the opposite end from where you start.

If you want to explore the top of Grandfather Mountain without hiking up the strenuous Profile Trail through Grandfather Mountain State Park (see Chapter 5), pay the entrance fee to enter the private attraction operated by the Grandfather Mountain Stewardship Foundation. You can easily spend an afternoon visiting the famous Mile High Swinging Bridge; the Wilson Center for Nature Discovery; the wildlife habitat discovery area with cougars, black bears, bald eagles, river otters, and elk; and hiking the rugged mountaintop trails without scaling the mountain from the base. The entrance is located at 2050 Blowing Rock Hwy., Linville, NC 28646.

Trail Tip: Stay on the designated trail and don't be tempted to cut switchbacks, which are designed to minimize erosion. Taking the shortcut contributes to the problem. Similarly, go through the puddles and mud, rather than around them, to not widen the trail.

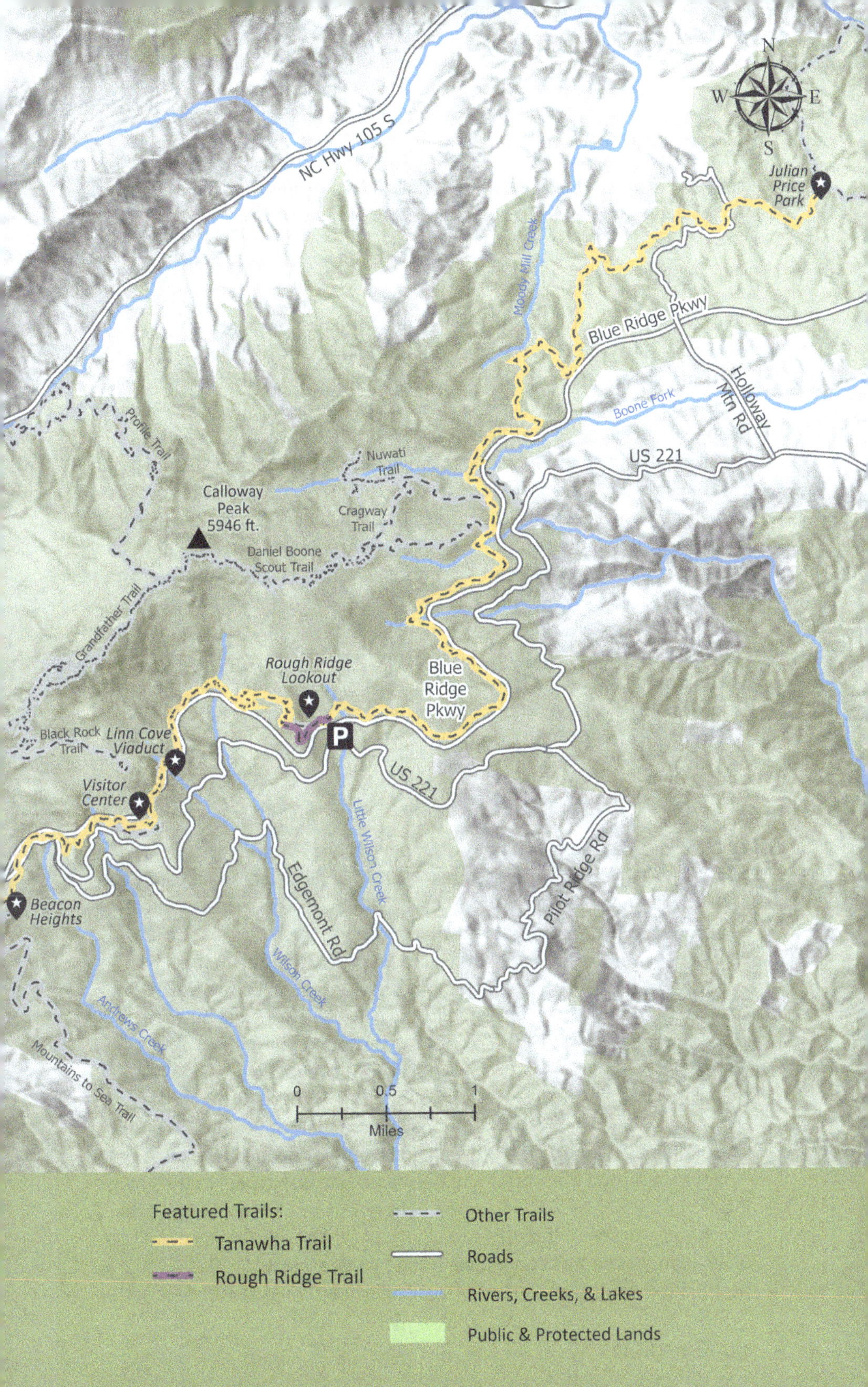

N
W E
S
NC Hwy 105 S
Julian Price Park
Blue Ridge Pkwy
Holloway Mtn Rd
Moody Mill Creek
Boone Fork
US 221
Profile Trail
Nuwati Trail
Cragway Trail
Calloway Peak 5946 ft.
Daniel Boone Scout Trail
Grandfather Trail
Rough Ridge Lookout
Blue Ridge Pkwy
Black Rock Trail
Linn Cove Viaduct
P
US 221
Visitor Center
Little Wilson Creek
Pilot Ridge Rd
Beacon Heights
Edgemont Rd
Wilson Creek
Andrews Creek
Mountains to Sea Trail
0   0.5   1
Miles
Featured Trails:
Tanawha Trail
Rough Ridge Trail
Other Trails
Roads
Rivers, Creeks, & Lakes
Public & Protected Lands

Hungry? Let's Eat!

Blowing Rock is a favorite destination for a treat after experiencing the amazing views on the Rough Ridge Trail. Additional Blowing Rock treats can be found in Chapter 7, Green Knob Trail at Sims Pond.

The Speckled Trout Restaurant and Bottle Shop
922 Main St., Blowing Rock, NC 28605

The Speckled Trout is a welcome respite for lunch or dinner after a day outdoors. Owned by a sister duo, this community-oriented business is a local treasure. Their restaurant features regional dishes (Appalachian fare) with a rotating seasonal menu and sources local ingredients. Carolina Mountain Trout is of course the featured dish. They prepare it many ways, with a long list of Southern side dishes to choose from, such as smoked Gouda grits, Hoppin' John, and moonshine-glazed carrots. Soups, salads, sandwiches, and other entrées will equally entice you. Chef Michael Foreman is a "trailblazer for the culinary movement in the High Country." In addition to an outstanding menu, The Speckled Trout "promotes beer and wine producers who take a thoughtful approach to practice and ingredients." Their drink menu houses a full list of cocktails, an extensive wine list, and many beer options. Catch "Tunes at the Trout," featuring High Country musicians every Thursday from 6 to 8 p.m. Check online for schedule. Indoor and outdoor seating is available. Since it's popular, reservations are strongly recommended, but walk-ins are welcome. Closed on Tuesday and Wednesday.

Blue Deer Cookies on Main
960 Main St. Ste. 3, Blowing Rock, NC 28605

This cookie, ice cream, and coffee shop will satisfy your post-trail sweet tooth. Their made-to-order ice cream sandwich is a tasty treat, especially on a hot day. Or just have a scoop of ice cream or a cookie solo. Blue Deer

bakes their cookies fresh daily and sources Homeland Creamery Ice Cream from the Piedmont and Local Lion Coffee from Boone. Established in 2018, the original Blue Deer camper can be found serving customers along US Hwy. 321 S. between Blowing Rock and Boone during the warm months. There is one additional location in Boone, Blue Deer on King. Check online for hours. The Blowing Rock and Boone locations are open 7 days a week, and both offer a full espresso bar. If stopping at the camper location on US Hwy. 321 S., be sure to check out the Middle Fork Greenway, which has a trailhead there. Eventually, the Middle Fork Greenway will be a 6.5-mile multi-use trail connecting Boone to Blowing Rock. This section will be 2 miles long by the summer of 2024, reaching Tweetsie Railroad.

Green Knob Trail at Sims Pond

Distance: **2.3 miles, loop**
Difficulty Level: **moderate**
Trailhead: **Blue Ridge Parkway, Milepost 295.9/ Sims Pond Overlook**

You're off to great places, today is your day.
Your mountain is waiting, so get on your way.
— Dr. Seuss

ocated on the Blue Ridge Parkway close to Julian Price Memorial Park is a family-friendly loop trail that is a hidden gem. It hits all the highlights of the area: thickets of rhododendron, wildflowers, rocky stream crossings, and to finish it all off, an impressive view of Grandfather Mountain.

This hike is best experienced in the counterclockwise direction from the Sims Pond Overlook. After skirting the edge of this small but picturesque pond, the trail gently winds through the woods following the rocky Sims Creek, passing several small waterfalls. There are a couple of creek crossings where you need to choose your rocks carefully to keep your feet dry. The trail then goes under the towering Sims Creek Viaduct, and from there, gradually climbs up to a scenic open pasture after passing through a cattle gate. You will find a sweet little bench for a rest under a shade tree in the middle of the pasture. Then the trail continues to climb up to the top of Green Knob, which peaks at an elevation of 3,920 feet. Look for the historic stone directional arrows to keep you on the trail.

The way back down is relatively steep and opens up into a small wild-flower meadow close to the bottom with an imposing view of Grandfather Mountain. From there, it's a short walk back to the start, after crossing the Parkway just south of the Sims Pond Overlook parking lot.

More to Know

Green Knob Trail is part of Julian Price Memorial Park. The main part of the park is located a short distance south on the Parkway around Milepost 297. The park is named for Julian Price, an insurance executive from Greensboro, who purchased 4,200 acres in this area as a recreational retreat for his employees. His family donated the land to the Blue Ridge Parkway after his death in 1946. Sims Pond, created by an earth and stone dam on Sims Creek, was originally built to raise rainbow trout for Price Lake. Although it is no longer used for this purpose, it is regularly stocked with trout, and fishing is allowed with the proper North Carolina fishing license.

Running Thoughts

Enjoy the beauty along the trail's ever-changing landscape. There is so much to take in. Consider the first mile or so along the creek as a warm-up at a gentle pace. As you enter the cow pasture, sweep down into the field, and use the climb up Green Knob for hill repeats. Jog or walk back down, repeating the section a few times if you wish. Take a little water break and breather, then complete the route back to the Sims Pond parking area at a cooldown pace. Watch your footing on the steep return.

Getting There

The trailhead is located on the Blue Ridge Parkway at Milepost 295.9. There is a small, paved parking area at the Sims Pond Overlook where the trail begins. A trail map is located next to the parking lot. No restrooms available.

Extend Your Trip

Julian Price Memorial Park offers a variety of activities, including an extensive and scenic picnic area along Wylie Creek with permanent restrooms (closed in winter), a large campground, and boat rentals for Price Lake. There are several spectacular trails in Julian Price Memorial Park, including two loop trails: the moderately strenuous 5.5-mile Boone Fork Trail, accessible from the campground and the picnic area; and the easy 2.7-mile Price Lake Trail that loops around the edge of this pristine lake, accessible at the Price Lake Overlook (Milepost 296.7).

Also nearby is Moses H. Cone Memorial Park at Milepost 294, with the grand Flat Top Manor. Built in Colonial Revival style in 1901 by the prosperous Cone family from Greensboro as a country estate, the Manor is magnificently positioned overlooking the vast mountain vista. The Southern Highland Craft Guild has a small store in the manor, with seasonal craft demonstrations on the wide front porch. The park has several trails, including a 20-minute loop trail around Flat Top Manor, a 2.6-mile trail up to an observation tower on top of Flat Top Mountain, and 25 miles of well-maintained carriage trails, gently winding through fields and forests down to Bass Lake. The lake is encircled by a beautiful, flat, carriage-width, 1-mile trail with its own parking lot and entrance.

Hungry? Let's Eat!

Are you ready to eat after your hike/run, but not ready to leave the Parkway? Julian Price Memorial Park offers many picnic tables in a picturesque setting.

Trail Tip: *No matter how much you plan, the weather can prove the forecast wrong. Unexpected and sudden storms or rain showers are common, especially in the mountains, but you can prepare for surprises. To solve this problem, pack lightweight rain gear.*

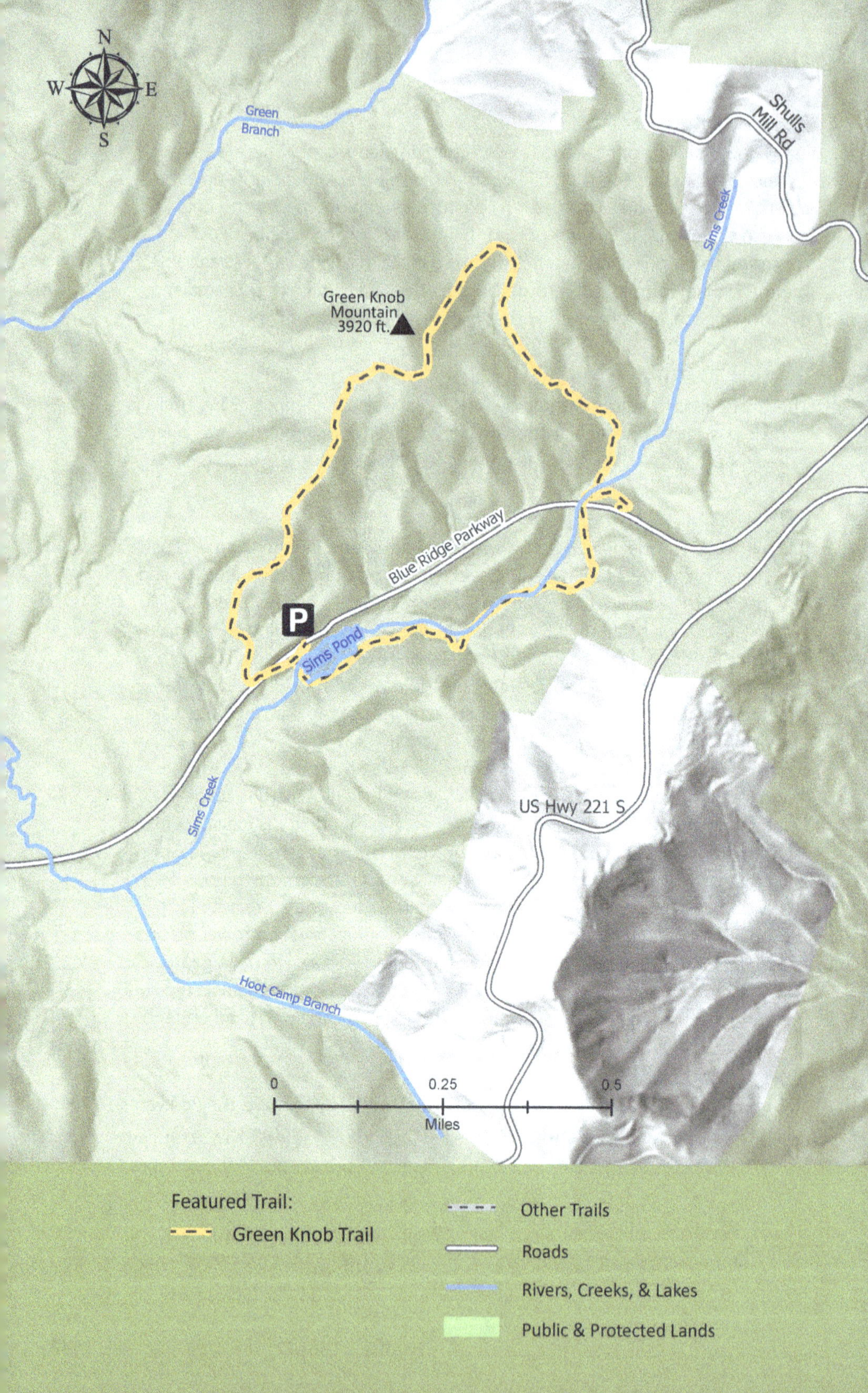

N
W E
S
Green Branch
Shulls Mill Rd
Sims Creek
Green Knob Mountain 3920 ft.
Blue Ridge Parkway
P
Sims Pond
Sims Creek
US Hwy 221 S
Hoot Camp Branch
0
0.25
0.5
Miles
Featured Trail:
Green Knob Trail
Other Trails
Roads
Rivers, Creeks, & Lakes
Public & Protected Lands

Blowing Rock is a charming village located a short, 3-mile drive away, full of many shops and restaurant choices. A couple of options are listed below, with more choices in Chapter 6 (Rough Ridge and Tanawha Trail). Don't miss a visit to the Memorial Park in the middle of town. Equipped with a playground, a gazebo, tennis courts, basketball courts, a picnic area, and public restrooms, it's a lovely spot to relax, breathe in cool mountain air, and bask in the sunshine. Remember, weekends can get crowded in Blowing Rock, so be patient when looking for parking. We unfortunately don't have any secret parking spots to suggest, but encourage you to go at off-times or in the off-season.

Six Pence Pub
1121 Main St., Blowing Rock, NC 28605

Relax and enjoy traditional American and British comfort food inside at cozy pub tables, outside on the side patio decorated with colorful flags and umbrella tables, or in the long barroom with rustic wood floors and pressed tin ceiling. Try the fish and chips, bangers and mash, or other traditional dishes from across the pond. Soups, salads, sandwiches, and burgers, as well as rotating daily features, round out the menu. To accompany your meal, there are many beers on tap. The wait staff is friendly, attentive, and ready to serve at this family-owned restaurant. Six Pence is a welcomed stop after a day of fresh air and time on the trail. Closed on Thursday. If you're ever in the historic district of Savannah, Georgia, visit the other Six Pence Pub.

Blowing Rock Market
990 Main St., Blowing Rock, NC 28605

Need a quick stop for a hot breakfast sandwich before the trails, or a made-to-order deli sandwich post-hike? Blowing Rock Market is your go-to! At this local corner market, open 7 days a week, you will find everything from coffee, craft beers, and wines, to homemade cinnamon rolls, muffins, and other locally baked sweet treats, or build-your-own sandwich orders with Boar's Head meats. Stop by in the afternoon and chill at a picnic table out front with a locally sourced ice cream sandwich or other frozen delights from their freezer case. Check out their fresh or frozen premade meals, a quick answer to dinner. Stay tuned for a second location, Mountaineer Market, coming soon in Boone.

Summit Trail, Elk Knob State Park

Distance: **3.8 miles, round trip, out and back**
Difficulty Level: **strenuous**
Trailhead: **5564 Meat Camp Rd., Todd, NC 28684**

*Forget not that the earth delights to feel your bare feet
and the winds long to play with your hair.*
— Khalil Gibran

Elk Knob State Park is a treasure in northwest North Carolina. Located just outside of Boone near the unusually named community of Meat Camp, close to the Tennessee border, Elk Knob is one of the highest peaks in the High Country. The Summit Trail gradually takes you through a northern hardwood forest to the top with 961 feet of elevation gain. At the 5,520-foot elevation, you will enjoy spectacular views from two different points: north toward The Peak, Mount Rogers, Three Top, Bluff Mountain, and Mount Jefferson; and south toward Grandfather Mountain, Mount Mitchell, and the Roan Highlands. Ranked by the State Park as moderately challenging, the trail is well designed (built by volunteers!), well maintained, and suitable for all ages.

The views are incredible any time of year, but, as is typical in the mountains, the summit can be in the clouds on some days. Look for spring wildflowers, including flame azaleas, and some of the best bluet patches around, and endless views of bright colors in the fall. You may be surprised to find a snowy wonderland during winter months.

More to Know

Elk Knob is part of the Amphibolite Mountains, an unusual cluster of high peaks north of Boone. The Amphibolites are named for a calcium-rich and rare metamorphic rock that forms rich soils when it breaks down, providing a special habitat for uncommon plant and animal species. Trees near the summit are short but can be well over 100 years old, stunted by the harsh conditions. Look for the colorful lichen everywhere. This high peak is the source for the North Fork of the New River, the world's second oldest river, which flows north through Virginia and West Virginia, eventually reaching the Ohio and Mississippi Rivers.

Running Thoughts

It is a vigorous climb to Elk Knob's summit and a very good hill workout. The trail's well-designed switchbacks and well-maintained, single-track trail surface makes running to the lookout extremely pleasurable. The mileage is clearly marked every 0.5 miles. Once at the top, enjoy the view from both the north and south lookout points. If running up is not in your workout plan for the day, give the other trails in the park a try.

Getting There

Elk Knob State Park is a 20-minute drive from Boone. Follow NC Hwy. 194 north to Meat Camp Road, which winds 5.5 miles through a beautiful High Country valley with spectacular views of the surrounding mountains. Look for the large State Park sign. There are restrooms at the picnic area.

Extend Your Trip

Although the Summit Trail is the most popular trail in Elk Knob State Park, there are several other trails. These include the 2-mile Backcountry Trail, which leads to some primitive campsites and a group camping area. The 1-mile Beech Tree Trail loops around the picnic area and is a Kids in Parks TRACK Trail, which means kids can earn prizes for completing and tracking this hike. Check kidsinparks.com for more information. The future 40-mile Northern Peaks State Trail will connect Boone to West Jefferson through Elk Knob State Park.

If you want to extend your time in the High Country, consider exploring by bike. The small community of Todd offers a gorgeous route along Railroad Grade Road, originally the rail line for the Virginia Creeper. The 10-mile corridor from Todd to Fleetwood is quite scenic. You'll have views of the South Fork of the New River along the entire route, and you will pass many picturesque hillside Christmas tree farms along this flat, smooth road, with very light, local traffic. Todd Island Park and River Access, located at 1219 Todd Railroad Grade Rd., is 2.75 miles outside of Todd and has a gravel parking lot, portable toilets, and river access. It is a good starting point for your bike ride. A well-crafted pedestrian bridge takes you over to an island in the river. Or start your ride in Todd proper, near Cook Memorial Park, where you can enjoy a picnic afterward. Depending on your parking choice, your round-trip ride is 15–20 miles.

Hungry? Let's Eat!

Home to the Appalachian State Mountaineers, Boone is a not-to-miss destination, with delicious casual dining options in and around town. We feature several notable choices. Also, check out two other favorites: Melanie's for brunch and lunch (closes at 2 p.m.), and Proper for its Southern fare with a "modern, seasonal slant" (opens at 4 p.m., Thursday through Sunday).

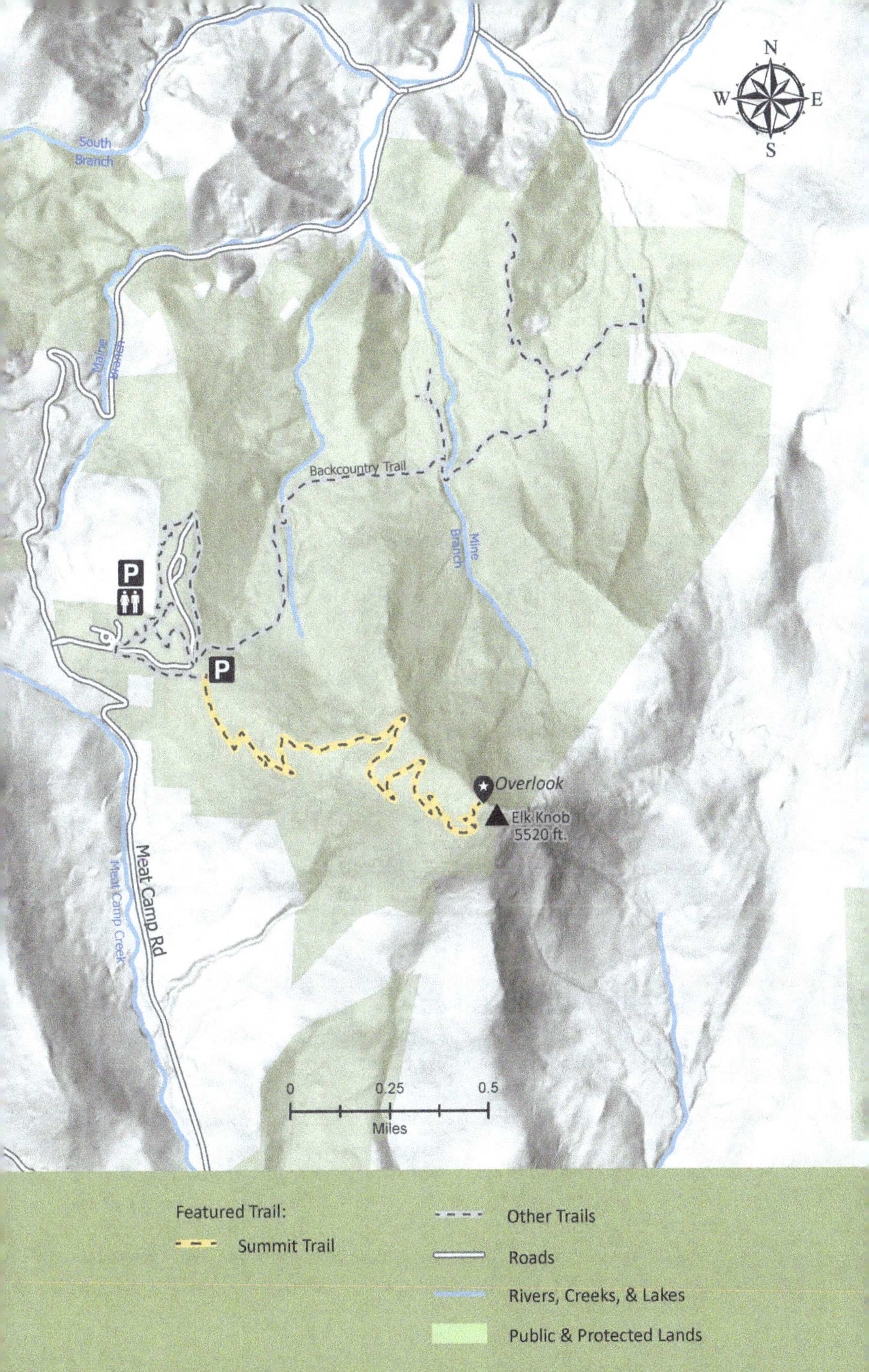

N
W E
S
South Branch
Beaver
Backcountry Trail
Mine Branch
P
P
Meat Camp Rd
Meat Camp Creek
Overlook
Elk Knob
5520 ft.
0
0.25
0.5
Miles
Featured Trail:
Summit Trail
Other Trails
Roads
Rivers, Creeks, & Lakes
Public & Protected Lands

Wild Craft Eatery
506 W. King St., Boone, NC 28607

This sweet Boone establishment serves up "good mood food" and appeals to carnivores and vegetarians alike. Try the Tempeh Gouda Tacos, Cuban Beans and Rice, Wild Mahi Sandwich, or the Watauga Farm Burger. On the lighter side, their soup and salads are equally satisfying. Serving lunch and dinner on their front covered patio or inside at cozy tables, they make sure a meal any time of year is pleasing. Wild Craft Eatery uses wholesome, local, fresh ingredients, sourcing from North Carolina farms to create comfort foods from all American cultures: "Locally Crafted, Wildly Delicious." Pet- and kid-friendly, this place is a gem. If busy, it's worth the wait. They are closed on Tuesday and Wednesday.

Booneshine Brewing
465 Industrial Park Dr., Boone, NC 28607

Booneshine got its start with the brewery in 2015 and today includes a tasting room and a restaurant. "Make Boone Shine" is their mission and shine it does! The atmosphere is lively and friendly, with bar seating, plenty of indoor tables, as well as a large outdoor patio and beer garden. Visit around the fire pit, enjoy trivia night, play a little cornhole, and order up some lunch or dinner to go with one of the many Booneshine craft brews. Choose from a vast array of sandwiches, burgers, flatbreads, salads, and appetizers (called Smalls), as well as a kid's menu. Booneshine prides itself on offering locally sourced products. It's a great place to relax and refuel in the High Country! Closed on Monday.

Stick Boy Kitchen
211 Boone Heights Dr., Boone, 28607

You may have seen Stick Boy mentioned on the menu in area restaurants. Their bakery items and desserts are locally famous. In business since 2001, its original location and production bakery across the street from Appalachian State University serves baked goods and smoothies. It also offers a full espresso bar. The Kitchen, as it is referred to by locals, opened in 2013 after needing to expand. This place is a crowd pleaser and can take care of your post-trail hunger. The cleverly named menu items will keep you amused as you peruse the multitude of delicious options. A breakfast menu (served all day), hot and cold sandwiches, soups, salads, and of course their breads and baked goods are offered Monday through Saturday. The Bakery and Kitchen create from scratch with quality ingredients and without additives or preservatives. We appreciate their commitment to serving the High Country through their love of food!

CAROLINE'S GRANOLA

Caroline's granola is a sweet and healthy treat that can be enjoyed in many ways. It can be eaten as cereal with milk, as a topping or layers for a yogurt and fruit parfait, or just as a pick-me-up snack during your hike. The nuts, oats, seeds, and dried fruits will keep your tummy happy and your energy level up as you exercise.

INGREDIENTS:

3 ½ cups rolled oats
½ cup coconut flakes, unsweetened
3 tablespoons sesame seeds
¼ cup sunflower seeds or pumpkin seeds
1 cup chopped walnuts or sliced almonds
2 teaspoons cinnamon
1 teaspoon sea salt
½ teaspoon nutmeg
¼ cup brown sugar
¼ cup canola oil
2 tablespoons honey
1 tablespoon maple syrup
2 teaspoons vanilla
2 cups raisins or dried cranberries

DIRECTIONS:

Preheat the oven to 375°F. Combine all ingredients in a large bowl, except dried fruit. The best way to mix Is with clean hands (it will be sticky, but just keep going). Line a cookie sheet with foil. Spread mixture evenly on foil. Bake for 5 minutes, stir, then bake for another 8–10 minutes. Don't over-bake. It crisps up as it cools completely. If it isn't crispy enough when cooled, bake it a few more minutes. Mix in dried fruit. Store in an airtight container at room temperature. If not using immediately, granola can be stored in the freezer for several months.

Stone Mountain Loop Trail, Stone Mountain State Park

Distance: **4.5 miles, loop**
Difficulty Level: **strenuous**
Trailhead: **3042 Frank Pkwy., Roaring Gap, NC 28668**

I took a walk in the woods and came out taller than trees.
— Henry David Thoreau

The Stone Mountain Loop Trail hits the three top highlights of Stone Mountain State Park: the 600-foot open-face, granite summit of Stone Mountain; the historic Hutchinson Homestead; and the spectacular 200-foot Stone Mountain Falls. Although a challenging hike with more than 900 feet of elevation gain and multiple sets of stairs, the payoff is well worth the effort, and it is a good choice for those interested in a bit of a challenge.

We recommend starting at the Upper Trailhead parking lot, where you can take the trail counterclockwise (get to the summit first) or clockwise (get to the waterfalls first). The best lunch/snack spots are either on the summit, where there are wide open spaces and stunning views of the Piedmont, or at the grassy homestead area. The trail also passes through rhododendron thickets and lush ferns and crosses a small stream several times. At this stream you have a fun option to rock hop or take a footbridge, offering a wide variety of trail experiences for your adventure. As you walk through the grassy meadows at the base of Stone Mountain, be sure to keep a lookout for climbers on the rock face. The portion of the Loop Trail following the creek near the base of the mountain is part of the NC Mountains-to-Sea Trail.

The historic Hutchinson Homestead demonstrates what life was like for settlers in the mid-1800s, complete with a log cabin, barn, blacksmith shop, corncrib, and original furnishings. The log cabin is open on weekends during the peak season. If you want to add fishing to your day, the park offers 20 miles of trout streams (valid permits required).

More to Know

Stone Mountain is named for its expansive exposed granite dome, which is a National Natural Landmark, and impressively rises above the surrounding area. Called a pluton, this igneous rock, formed by lava below the Earth's surface, is estimated to be 300 million years old. Wind and water over the years have carved what looks like stripes on the rock's surface. From the top, the granite has the unique appearance of the moon's cratered surface. The imposing rock face can be seen for miles.

Running Thoughts

Stone Mountain Loop allows you to vary your workout throughout the trail due to extreme changes in terrain. There are shaded and/or flat sections along the stream, open grass areas near the homestead, as well as challenging switchbacks and stairs to the summit and waterfall. Consider starting from the Upper Trailhead parking lot, running in a clockwise direction. Take in the scenic waterfall as you come down more than 250 stairs. Departing the falls, run at an easy-to-moderate pace. As you approach the open field at the base of the mountain, explore the homestead and take a water break. When ready, wind your way to the switchbacks and stairs leading to the summit,

and consider this a stadium stair workout. Try to keep a steady pace up to the top (you know what's right for you). Your reward is a impressive rock top summit with amazing views. This is a great rest spot after your hard-earned climb. Catch your breath, explore the rock surface, have an energy snack and water from your running pack or belt, and then wind your way back down to the parking lot at an easy pace, completing the loop.

Getting There

Enter Stone Mountain State Park and follow Frank Parkway to the Upper Trailhead parking area, where there are restrooms and picnic tables. You can also follow Frank Parkway for another 2 miles to the Lower Trailhead parking area, where there are also restrooms.

Extend Your Trip

If you are interested in seeing more waterfalls in the park and adding a little more distance to your hike, you can take the Middle Falls/Lower Falls Trail from the Stone Mountain Loop Trail (1 mile to Lower Falls, 2-mile round trip). You can also park at the Widow's Creek Trailhead, which is 1 mile past the Lower Trailhead parking area, and walk a few hundred feet to get to Widow's Creek Falls, a popular swimming hole. If you are wanting a bit more distance and more expansive views of the Blue Ridge mountains, try adding in the loop with Wolf Rock and Cedar Rock Trails (2.5 miles total).

For an even longer day, Carter Falls near Elkin is a short and terrific little hike (1-mile loop) with a 60-foot cascading waterfall on Big Elkin Creek. The parking lot is well marked and is located on Pleasant Ridge Road where Martin Byrd Road ends near Byrd's Branch Campground.

Hungry? Let's Eat!

Stone Mountain Country Store
1050 John P. Frank Pkwy., Traphill, NC 28685
After a long hike or run, Stone Mountain Country Store is the perfect place to rest and recharge with generous servings of hand-dipped ice cream and burgers and dogs hot off the grill. Located right outside the park, the store is

N
W E
S
Widow's Creek Falls
P
P
Lower Trailhead
Stone Mountain Rd
Stone Mountain Creek
Wolf Rock Trail
Widows Creek Trail
Hutchinson Homestead
Stone Mountain 2305 ft.
Wolf Rock
Cedar Rock Trail
Cedar Rock
Mountains-to-Sea Trail
P
Upper Trailhead
Black Jack Ridge Trail
Stone Mountain Falls
Stone Mountain Rd
Middle Falls/ Lower Falls Trail
Bridle Loop Trail
Bridle Out- and-Back Trail
Big Sandy Creek
Little Sandy Creek
Longbottom Rd
Frank Pkwy
0
0.5
1
Miles
Featured Trail:
Stone Mountain Loop Trail
Other Trails
Roads
Rivers, Creeks, & Lakes
Public & Protected Lands

an easy stop. Be sure to check out local arts and crafts on-site. There are also some fishing and camping provisions for purchase. We especially love the big front porch and rocking chairs to sit and relax with your treats.

Chez Joséphine Restaurant
115 Bordeaux Ln., Traphill, NC 28685

If you are looking for something a little more upscale, Chez Joséphine at Roaring River Vineyards is a great find, with an attractive deck overlooking the river, offering small plates, soups, salads, paninis, and desserts, and of course wine tastings (locally brewed beer too). Not to worry, you'll fit right in with comfortable outdoor attire. Open Thursday through Sunday.

Stone Mountain State Park is close to Elkin, known as a trail town, where there are dozens of options for delicious treats and multiple ways to conclude your day. Here are a couple of our favorites.

The Reeves Theater & Café
129 W. Main St., Elkin, NC 28621

This unique venue serves up mouth-watering sandwiches, salads, and other farm-to-table fare in their café. Partnering with local farmers and vendors in the Yadkin Valley, Reeves strives to be as sustainable as possible. If you come on the right day, acoustic music and other performances in the evenings are options, including a weekly open mic night if you are up for the challenge or just want to listen. A stop at the Theater could be just the right way to end your day! Open Wednesday through Saturday.

Grassy Creek Vineyard & Winery
235 Chatham Cottage Ln., State Road, NC 28676

The Yadkin Valley region is known for its wineries, and Grassy Creek is one of the best. This former dairy farm has converted a stable into a cozy and attractive tasting room with an excellent selection of wines. Child- and pet-friendly, the winery offers a lovely outdoor seating area that includes a large fire pit and cornhole boards, and there is often live music and food trucks on the weekends. The vineyard has access to the NC Mountains-to-Sea Trail to extend your adventures. Closed on Tuesday and Wednesday.

10 Salem Lake Trail

Distance: **7 miles, loop**
Difficulty Level: **easy**
Trailhead: **815 Salem Lake Rd. or Linville Rd. S.E., Winston-Salem, NC 27107**

Nature does not hurry, yet everything is accomplished.
— Lao Tzu

S alem Lake Trail winds around the perimeter of Salem Lake on a well-packed, shaded, carriage-width dirt path that is ideal for runners, cyclists, hikers, dog walkers, and equestrians, with scenic views of the water at almost every turn.

This popular trail is well marked with mile markers in a counterclockwise direction, starting at the playground and picnic area near the main parking lot at the marina on Salem Lake Road. The trail is mostly flat but includes a few hills for a little challenge. Beautiful all times of the year with continuous lake views, this popular trail is a peaceful respite from the hustle and bustle of the Triad. Sunsets and sunrises are especially gorgeous. Park benches with views of the lake are perfect stops for snacks or water breaks and time to reflect and catch your breath.

Even though this is a very popular destination on weekends and the parking lots may look full, the trail doesn't feel crowded because of its wide width and long length. We do encourage a visit during the week, as you will notice more wildlife, such as turtles sunning on logs, a heron at the water's edge, and sights and sounds of many other waterfowl. You will most certainly spot small fishing boats and kayaks, especially in the early morning.

More to Know

Salem Lake was originally created in 1911 when a dam was constructed across Salem Creek. The current dam, the third one built, was constructed in 1931. The trail has a 9-station Bike TRACK Trail for kids. Each station features interpretive information about the plants and animals in and around Salem Lake, some information about the importance of clean water, and tips to improve biking skills.

Running Thoughts

This is a perfect trail for your weekly long run. Salem Lake Trail is mostly flat and wide, and it provides a shaded canopy where you can easily get 7 miles solo or with friends. Include a stop at the parking lot at 3.5 miles (either end) for a sip of water at the fountain, or a quick stop at the restroom. Want more mileage? Take two laps, or extend your route on the Salem

Creek Greenway that winds toward Winston-Salem. The greenway connects into the trail not far from the dam and marina. There is a stream crossing if you choose to follow the Salem Creek Greenway, where your feet may get wet.

Getting There

There are two parking options for Salem Lake Trail. The main entrance near the Salem Lake Marina Center offers larger and more plentiful parking. It is also the best lot for disability access. The marina office building has restrooms as well as a bait shop, fishing pier, and boat and kayak rentals. The playground and another set of restrooms are located in the Point parking lot, to the right of the marina entrance on Salem Lake Road. The other option is the Linville Road lot. It is much smaller, but it still offers a restroom, water fountain, and one disabled parking spot, and it provides closer access to the trail if you are coming from the east.

Extend Your Trip

For a great day out on bicycles with your family or friends, you can park at Salem Lake, ride the path around the lake, then continue on the Salem Creek Greenway toward downtown Winston-Salem. When you get to Old Salem, you have several options. You can continue on the Salem Creek Greenway a little farther to visit the Gateway Nature Preserve. Another option is to turn north and follow the Strollway across Salem Parkway into downtown and stop for lunch at one of the many downtown restaurants or picnic in Bailey Park. Then follow the Long Branch Trail back to the Salem Creek Greenway and back to Salem Lake. This entire trip is about 20 miles.

Hungry? Let's Eat!

Winston-Salem has a vibrant and walkable downtown with numerous restaurants, bakeries, coffee shops, breweries, bookstores, and galleries. Home to NC School of the Arts, there are always exceptional musical and theater performances on the calendar. Look for the annual RiverRun International Film Festival, Bookmarks Festival, and the largest Earth Day celebration in the state.

Cugino Forno Pizzeria
486 N. Patterson Ave., Ste. 115, Winston-Salem, NC 27101

Cugino Forno Pizzeria, meaning "cousin oven," was formed by three Turkish cousins who fully immersed themselves in the art and craft of Neapolitan-style pizza by spending time in Naples learning from the world's greatest pizzaiolos. Their pizzas are made with many imported, high-quality, Italian ingredients, and are baked at 900 degrees in an Italian oven with stone from Mount Vesuvius, creating a truly authentic experience. This popular establishment,

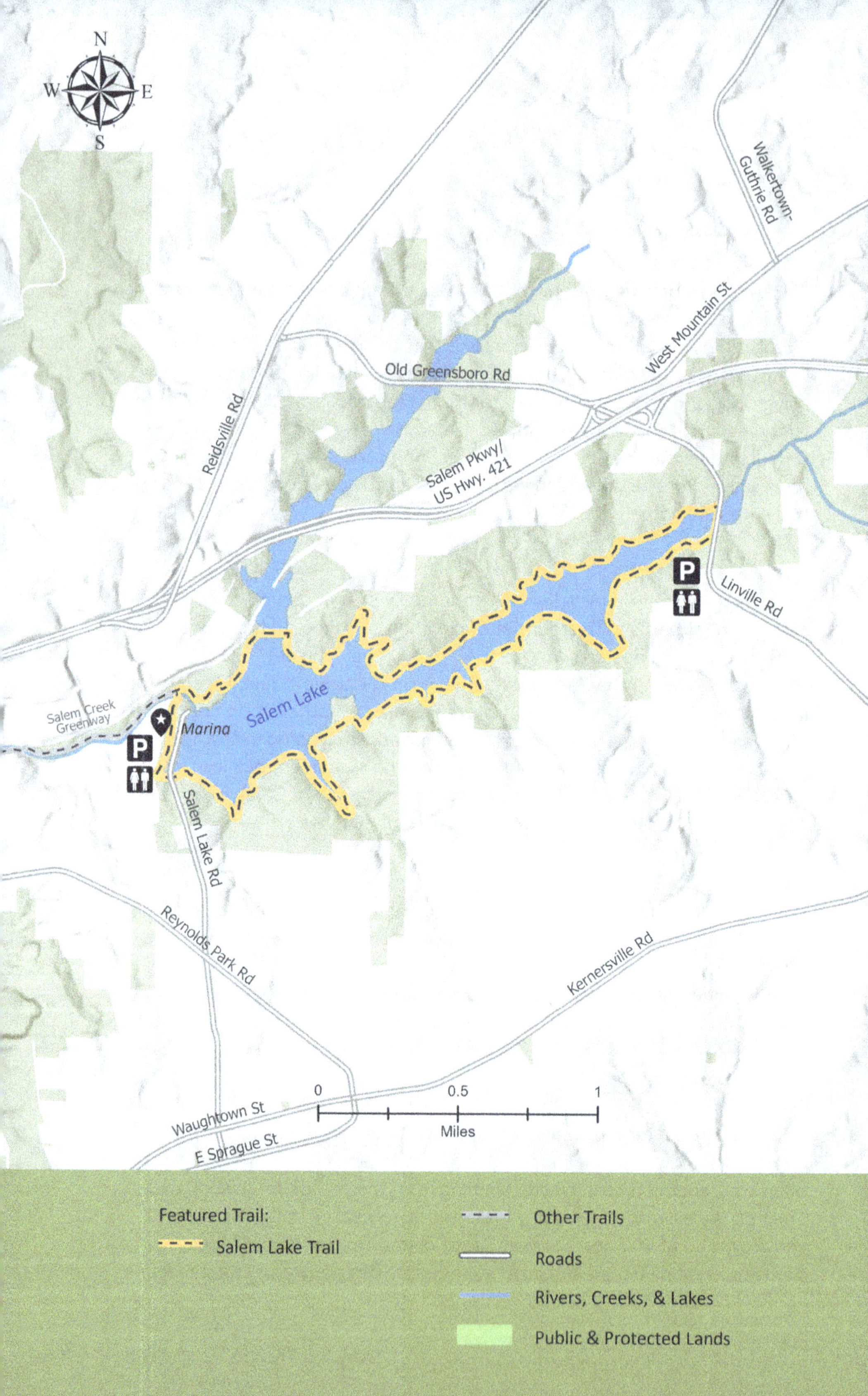

N
W E
S
Walkertown-Guthrie Rd
West Mountain St
Old Greensboro Rd
Salem Pkwy/ US Hwy. 421
Linville Rd
Reidsville Rd
Salem Creek Greenway
Marina
Salem Lake
Salem Lake Rd
Reynolds Park Rd
Kernersville Rd
Waughtown St
E Sprague St
0
0.5
1
Miles
Featured Trail:
Salem Lake Trail
Other Trails
Roads
Rivers, Creeks, & Lakes
Public & Protected Lands

adjacent to Bailey Park, is housed in a restored tobacco warehouse. There is indoor seating available, but the unique, outside patio is a treat all its own. Called the Coal Pit, after its origins as the coal pit for the historic power plant for R. J. Reynolds Tobacco Company, it is large and inviting with colorful picnic tables and attractive planters, and plenty of space for kids to play. With Cugino Forno located next to Incendiary Brewing Company, your beverage choice can pair nicely with your pizza. It is an ideal place to relax and refuel before returning to the trail. Cugino Forno's original location is in Greensboro. They have additional locations in Clemmons, Durham, and Wilmington.

Incendiary Brewing Company
486 N. Patterson Ave., Ste. 105, Winston-Salem, NC 27101

Conveniently positioned between Bailey Park and the Long Branch Greenway and next door to Cugino Forno, Incendiary Brewing Company is a local craft brewery. It was created by two Winston-Salem natives in 2018 after many years of brewing together and numerous homebrew competition successes. Brandon Branscome, John Bacon, and their crew are known for their IPAs and stouts. Look for their free CoalPitLive summer concert series from the end of May through September, featuring nationally known artists. Check schedules online or follow them on social media. You can also visit them at their Lewisville location, which offers rotating food trucks on-site and a weekly trivia night.

Piedmont Triad Farmers Market
2914 Sandy Ridge Rd., Colfax, NC 27235 (Exit #208 on I-40)

Located between Winston-Salem and Greensboro and open all week, this state-run, regional farmers market is fun to wander. Many local farmers and other vendors sell seasonal, fresh produce, homemade breads, cheeses, local meats, fresh fish, garden shrubs, plants, and gorgeous flower arrangements under covered, open-air market spaces. There's even an ice cream shop run by Wylin Grason Farms, located at the end of Farmers Area 2 (inside Building F) serving Homeland Creamery and Hershey's Ice Cream. If going solely for ice cream, check their hours and note they are closed on Monday and Tuesday. If you are exploring the full market grounds, be sure to check out A.B. Seed, a locally owned landscape and garden shop that is a unique indoor and outdoor experience. On weekends, the market often hosts craft fairs, car shows, garden events, and yoga classes, which might also draw you in. Occasionally, a road race starts and ends at the market. Check their website to see what's coming up!

Uwharrie Trail at Little Long Mountain

Distance: **4.4 miles to 6 miles, round trip, out and back**
Difficulty Level: **moderate**
Trailhead: **Jumping Off Rock Trailhead, 2015 Flint Hill Rd., Troy, NC 27371**

It is not so much for its beauty that the forest makes a claim upon men's hearts, as for that subtle something, that quality of air, that emanation from old trees, that so wonderfully changes and renews a weary spirit.

— Robert Louis Stevenson

The Uwharrie National Forest spans over 51,000 acres across multiple Piedmont counties, offering an abundance of trails, and is easily accessible from the Triad, Triangle, and Charlotte. The 40-mile long Uwharrie Trail is a National Recreation Trail and runs through the heart of Uwharrie National Forest from NC Hwy. 24/27 in the south near Troy to Tot Hill Farm Road in the north near Asheboro. Because of one small gap in the middle, the trail is not fully continuous.

Highlighted in this chapter is a segment of the Uwharrie National Recreation Trail that goes from the Jumping Off Rock Trailhead to Little Long Mountain. It offers one of the only scenic outlooks in the entire Uwharrie region. The trail begins on the opposite side of the road from the gravel parking area, just past the short bridge, and is marked by a small wooden sign. Heading north, after a quick ascent and descent, the trail follows Poison Fork Creek, one of the most pristine streams in the Piedmont, with small cascades and rock outcrops. You will need to rock hop across the stream, and in higher waters, you may get your feet wet. On the other side, you will be rewarded with a lush forest full of spring wildflowers and mountain laurel. Several different types of ferns, mosses, and lichens can also be spotted seasonally.

The ascent up Little Long Mountain leads you to the grassy bald, famous for its beautiful, 180-degree panoramic views of the surrounding mountains. Pause for lunch or a snack at the well-constructed Eagle's Nest shelter, built by Boy Scouts in 2015. This could be your turning point, or, after a water break with a view, carry on past the open bald and continue down the trail toward the Joe Moffitt Trailhead. On the way, you will come to an interesting area strewn with large white quartz boulders, a testament to the area's volcanic origins. If you choose to go all the way to Joe Moffitt Trailhead, the round trip is 6 miles.

More to Know

Once reaching as high as 20,000 feet, the Uwharrie Mountains are considered by some to be the oldest mountain range in the world, dating back 500 million years and now weathered away to elevations less than 1,100 feet. These mountains have a rich human history too, from Native peoples to America's first gold rush in the 1820s and 1830s. Completely cleared for farming and logging before becoming a National Forest in 1961, the Uwharries today have largely recovered and support a wide diversity of species.

Jumping Off Rock Trailhead has a story as well. It is named after an elevated flat rock outcropping overlooking the nearby Barnes Creek where, according to legend, a young Native American maiden jumped to her death when told her warrior had been killed in battle. When the warrior learned of his maiden's fate, he jumped to his death from the same rock.

Running Thoughts

Jog the first mile of the trail at a warm-up pace, cross the creek, then pick up your pace to the summit. Enjoy views atop the mountain, take in some water, and catch your breath. When ready, continue down to the Joe Moffitt Trailhead, turn, and run back up to the summit. The top of Little Long Mountain offers a flat, grassy space, as well as the covered platform shelter, making a peaceful spot for stretching or yoga. Catch a last view from up top and jog back down through the forest, back to the Jumping Off Rock Trailhead.

Getting There

The trailhead is on Flint Hill Road in the middle of Uwharrie National Forest, 30 minutes south of Asheboro and 20 minutes north of Troy. The shaded parking area is well marked. The trail begins across the road, just past the bridge, and is marked with a small, wooden sign. There are no restrooms.

Extend Your Trip

If you are looking for a little more distance, another trail choice is the 7-mile loop on Hannah's Creek Trail, Robbins Branch Trail, and the Birkhead Mountain Trail in the nearby Birkhead Mountains Wilderness. Park at the Robbins Branch Trailhead (5527 Lassiter Mill Rd., Asheboro, NC 27205). Although there are no vistas, the trail offers a great workout with several stream crossings to keep things interesting.

If you wish to add in cultural attractions, don't miss nearby Pisgah Covered Bridge, one of two remaining original, historic covered bridges in the state; and the small town of Seagrove, where more than 100 artists create famous, handmade, traditional pottery. The North Carolina Zoo, the world's largest natural habitat zoo, is also worth a visit.

Trail Tip: *Especially in the wilderness, pack a few key essentials for safety, including a pocketknife or multi-use tool, mini flashlight, battery pack for your phone, and first aid kit.*

N
W
E
S
Walkers Creek Trailhead
P
Lassiter Mill Rd
High Pine Church Rd
Eagles Field Rd
Pisgah Covered Bridge Rd
Uwharrie River
Uwharrie Trail
Poison Fork Creek
Burney Mill Rd
Abner Rd
King Mtn Rd
Joe Moffitt Trailhead
P
Grissom Rd
Little Long Mountain 922 ft.
Thayer Rd
Horseshoe Bend Rd
Barnes Creek
Low Water Bridge Rd
Love Joy Rd
Ophir Rd
Flint Hill Rd
Jumping Off Rock Trailhead
P
0   0.5   1
Miles
Tower Rd
Featured Trail:
Uwharrie Trail
Other Trails
Roads
Rivers, Creeks, & Lakes
Public & Protected Lands

Hungry? Let's Eat!

The Table
139 S. Church St., Asheboro, NC 27203
Warm and inviting, The Table is a place where owner Dustie Gregson wants
everyone to feel at home. The Asheboro native and her team created a space
where locals and visitors alike share not just delicious food, but community.
This old mill office building was brought back to life through Gregson's vision
and inspiration. The Table is an extremely popular destination for breakfast
and lunch. Menu items are perfectly created and thoughtfully plated. There
are also many coffee and bakery items to tempt you at the register. Seating is
available inside the light, airy space, or find a place on the front or side patios,
where beautiful plantings surround you. Closed on Sunday and Monday.

Four Saints Brewing
218 S. Fayetteville St., Asheboro, NC 27203
Featured as one of the best breweries in the South in 2022 by *Southern
Living* magazine, Four Saints Brewing is an ideal place to unwind and socialize
in a friendly, comfortable setting. Their knowledgeable staff can steer you
to just the right brew for your taste, with many award-winning varieties to
choose from, on tap and in cans. They even have seasonal favorites based
around stories of four different saints. "Great Beer for Great People" is their
mission, and they are ready to welcome you in and serve you and your trail
friends after your adventure. Closed on Monday.

Eldorado Outpost
4021 NC Hwy. 109, Troy, NC 27371
The eclectic Eldorado Outpost is in the remote heart of the Uwharrie
National Forest, providing traditional mercantile goods, clothing, and other
outdoor gear, as well as canoe and kayak rentals and other services for
outdoor adventurers. You can even get a hot meal, including breakfast biscuits,
hot-off-the-grill sandwiches, and chicken dinners, or cold drinks or a piece of
pie. The Outpost is a place you can get just about anything you may need!

Uwharrie Mercantile
401 N. Main St., Troy, NC 27371
In a historic downtown hotel, the Uwharrie Mercantile is worth the detour.
It offers homemade bakery items, soups, and sandwiches as well as a full
coffee bar, smoothies and lemonades/orangeades in a cozy, friendly space.
Shop for gifts such as jewelry, clothing, shoes, home decor, and body and
bath goods. The Mercantile is typically closed on Sunday and Monday.
Don't miss the Discover Uwharrie Welcome Center (100 W. Main St.) just
up the street.

Laurel Bluff Trail

Distance: **7 miles, round trip, out and back**
Difficulty Level: **moderate**
Trailhead: **5900 Block Lake Brandt Rd. or
5300 Block N. Church St., Greensboro, NC 27455**

The path reveals itself once you start walking.
— *Abhijit Naskar*

Extending above the southern shoreline of Lake Townsend between Lake Brandt Marina and North Church Street, the Laurel Bluff Trail is one of our favorites in the 40-plus mile network of Greensboro's Watershed Trails. This one is a little more challenging than some of the others, with some short, steep sections. But the lake and creek views, wetlands, and its namesake groves of mountain laurel make it extra special. Laurel Bluff is almost never crowded, and you might even have it mostly to yourself. An out-and-back trail, this is a fun hike for children, with several opportunities to get close to the water. There are highlights to each season: spring wildflowers, lush summer ferns, colorful fall foliage, and expansive forest views during the winter months. Bikes are not allowed, which makes it particularly attractive for hikers and runners.

More to Know

The Laurel Bluff Trail is part of the NC Mountains-to-Sea Trail, North Carolina's longest footpath, stretching almost 1,200 miles across the state from Clingmans Dome in the Great Smoky Mountains to Jockey's Ridge on the Outer Banks. It passes through 37 of North Carolina's 100 counties, climbs the tallest mountain peak (Mount Mitchell) and the highest sand dune (Jockey's Ridge) in the eastern US, and connects communities along the way. You can access the NC Mountains-to-Sea Trail in many different places across the state. For more information, check out mountainstoseatrail.org.

Running Thoughts

With a tree canopy almost always overhead, this single-track trail is a respite for the hot months, when shade is truly your friend. It is a challenge to run the sections that dip and climb. Watch your footing on some very rooty, rocky areas. Lower areas are perfect to get into a good, even running rhythm. A workout to consider on Laurel Bluff is running the first half at a warm-up pace, and on the return, run the second half faster (a negative split). Don't forget to stretch when you are finished!

Getting There

You can access the Laurel Bluff Trail from Lake Brandt Road or Church Street. If you park on Lake Brandt Road, look for a small parking lot next to the pump station, across the road from Lake Brandt Marina. If a restroom is

Trail Tip: Be on the lookout for snakes sunning on trails in warmer weather. Remember, we are in their territory. If you spot one, back away and wait for it to move off the trail, or detour around it. Don't try to scare it away or move it. Snakes don't want to waste their poison on humans but may strike/bite if they feel threatened.

required, make a stop at the marina. If you park on Church Street, look for the trailhead parking lot on the east side of Church Street (no restrooms at the Church Street Trailhead).

Extend Your Trip

The City of Greensboro manages more than 40 miles of trails around the watershed lakes: Lake Higgins, Lake Brandt, and Lake Townsend. Some of the trails are mountain bike trails, and others are for walking/running only. You can combine the Laurel Bluff Trail with the Reedy Fork Trail on the north side of Lake Townsend to create a 7.4-mile loop trail. The Reedy Fork Trail is a multi-use trail, so you might encounter mountain bikes.

Hungry? Let's Eat!

Giacomo's Italian Market
2109 New Garden Rd. E., Greensboro, NC 27410

Owner Giacomo Santomauro has a passion for his family-run business and wants customers to experience fresh, high-quality, Italian foods. You know when you walk inside that Giacomo's is authentic. The views from the counter —fresh-made sausage, salami, deli meats, marinated vegetables, cheeses, and antipasto—and the smells of all the foods prepared on-site are enough to make your mouth water. Their sandwiches, piled high with homemade deli meats and imported cheeses on homemade bread, are locally famous. A large board on the wall, hanging above the glass cases, lists cleverly named sandwich options. All sandwiches are carefully created and wrapped tightly in white butcher paper, making them easy to pack for your lunch on the trail. You might be tempted to take home a meal or dessert too! All are homemade with family recipes and there is a tradition of quality in everything they sell. You will want to come back! Closed on Monday and Tuesday.

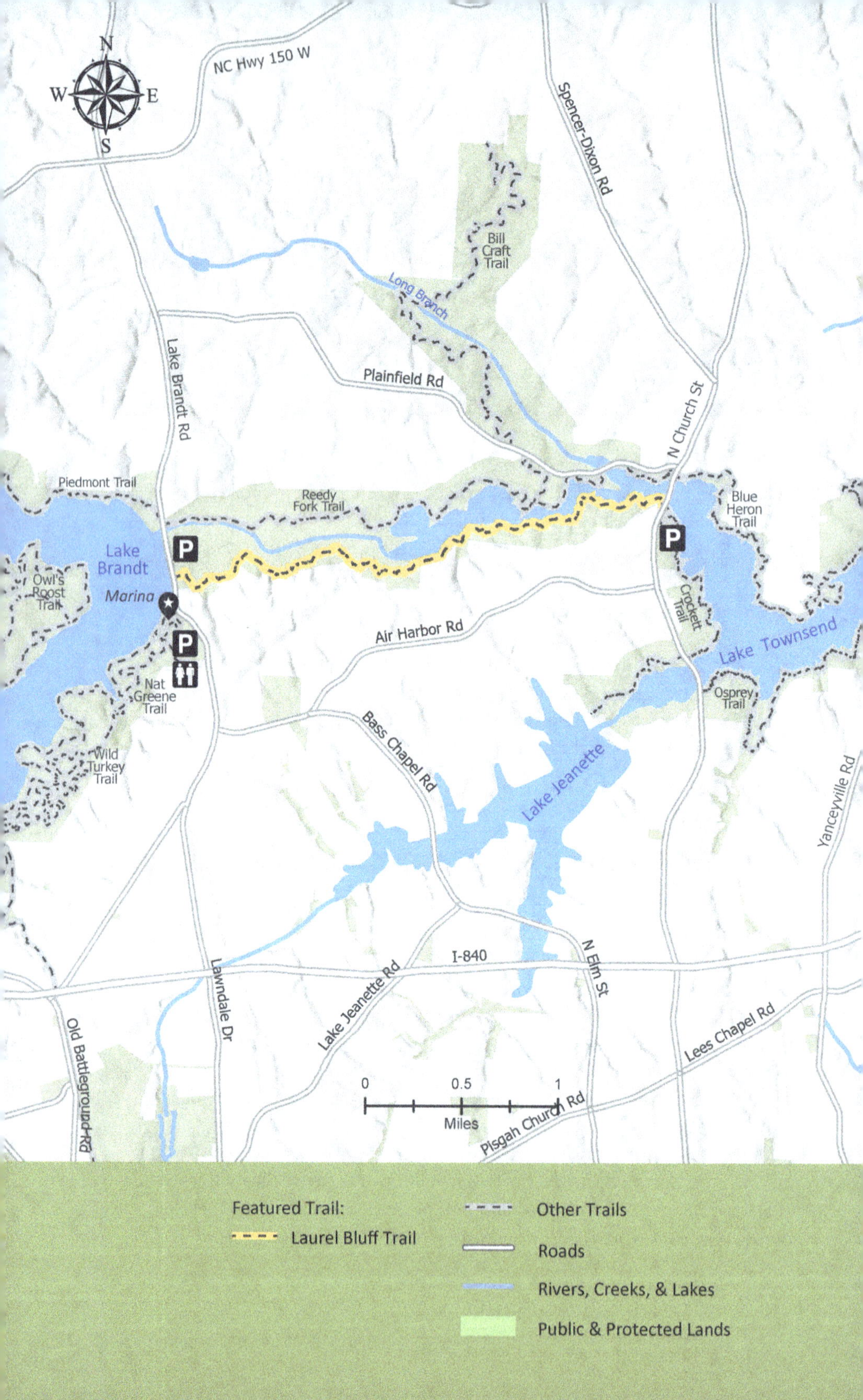

N
W E
S
NC Hwy 150 W
Spencer-Dixon Rd
Bill Craft Trail
Long Branch
Plainfield Rd
N Church St
Lake Brandt Rd
Piedmont Trail
Reedy Fork Trail
Blue Heron Trail
Lake Brandt
Marina
Owl's Roost Trail
P
P
Crockett Trail
Lake Townsend
Air Harbor Rd
Nat Greene Trail
Wild Turkey Trail
Osprey Trail
Bass Chapel Rd
Lake Jeanette
Yanceyville Rd
Lawndale Dr
Lake Jeanette Rd
I-840
N Elm St
Old Battleground Rd
Lees Chapel Rd
Pisgah Church Rd
0   0.5   1
Miles
Featured Trail:
Laurel Bluff Trail
Other Trails
Roads
Rivers, Creeks, & Lakes
Public & Protected Lands

Maxie B's
2403 Battleground Ave., Greensboro, NC 27408

Maxie B's began in 1985 as a frozen yogurt shop, with flair for home decor. Customers and staff enjoyed the cozy home feel that owner Robin Davis created. It was not your normal yogurt shop! For 16 years, frozen yogurt was the primary business. Then a little by accident, Robin started introducing her homemade cakes. Things took off and now, she and her team are focused solely on bakery items and are true masters of their trade. They make some of the best cakes, pies, cupcakes, and cookies in Greensboro from scratch with local ingredients. The menu has it all, from traditional favorites to creative

combinations, sold whole and by the slice, that are delicious and beautiful. Homemade dog treats are on the menu, too. If you are hiking with your four-legged friend, treat them to a "pupcake"! You can choose to sit in the shop's outdoor space, pleasantly surrounded by native plants, or in the cozy indoor parlor. Robin's commitment to sustainability shows up every-where, from green packaging to recycling and composting almost everything, including food and floral waste. Enjoy the total experience at Maxie B's! Closed on Sunday.

Juice Shop Smoothies
2146 Lawndale Dr., Greensboro, NC 27408

Juice Shop has been making refreshing fruit smoothies since 1996. This locally owned business is easy to spot, with its bright orange and green signage and cute polar bear logo (sipping on a smoothie of course). Juice Shop offers just one menu item in 10 delicious flavor combinations. Some of our favorites include: Raspberry Rush, Arctic Orange, and Cranberry Crush. With the purchase of your smoothie, selections include one addition if you wish: bee pollen, protein powder, or calcium. All smoothies are served in a 24-ounce size; however, they will split an order into two cups if you decide to share it. The friendly high school staff is almost as sweet as the smoothies. While you are waiting for your order, take a look at some of the recipients of their employee scholarships hanging on the shop wall, which date back to the beginning of the business. Juice Shop has two additional locations, one in Winston-Salem and another in Greensboro's Friendly Center.

Downtown Greenway, Greensboro

Distance: **4 miles, loop**
Difficulty Level: **easy**
Trailhead: **several parking options are available—Morehead Park at 475 Spring Garden St., Greensboro, NC 27401; Freedom Cornerstone at 750 Plott St., Greensboro, NC 27406; and on-street parking around the loop**

If you truly love nature, you will find beauty everywhere.
— *Vincent Van Gogh*

The Downtown Greenway is Greensboro's urban biking, running, and walking trail. It encircles the downtown area with 4 miles of an attractively landscaped, paved path, fully connecting the downtown to numerous neighborhoods and dozens of miles of trail networks in the city. Different from many other greenways, the Downtown Greenway features large, unique public art pieces created by nationally acclaimed artists that inspire, celebrate history, and are functional as benches, bike racks, and signs. The largest art pieces are at the four corners of the loop honoring Greensboro's unique history, including its role in the Revolutionary War; education; industry and textiles; and the civil rights movement. Each cornerstone is completely different.

In addition, a number of special features along the route will delight visitors while telling more stories. Take in the towering pottery cairns along the western side, or the interactive and colorful lighting under a railroad bridge, and the set of shapes mounted under another underpass based on old redlining maps. Altogether the art is phenomenal and authentically engaging to visitors. The Downtown Greenway is the only urban loop trail in North Carolina and one of only a few in the country.

More to Know

Adjacent to the Plott Street parking area is the Historic Magnolia House, which opened in 1949 as one of the only hotels between Atlanta and Richmond allowing African American travelers to stay overnight during segregation. The hotel was listed in *The Green Book*, an annually published travel guide that identified businesses safe for Black patrons. Today the Historic Magnolia House is a restored bed and breakfast with rooms decorated to reflect the 1950s and 60s eras, an event venue, and a restaurant serving traditional and delicious soul food dishes for lunch, dinner, and weekend brunches. Try one of their chef-inspired cocktails! Check restaurant hours before going.

Running Thoughts

There are many ways to vary your workout on the Downtown Greenway, so feel free to get creative! If you've never been on the loop, try a nice, easy 4 miles, taking time to study the art along the route. This is perfect for any level of runner needing to get in a few miles on a fairly flat, paved surface. If you want to try a more intense workout, use the four cornerstones as pace change locations. Warm up by running to a cornerstone, then pick up speed and run at a pushed pace to the next cornerstone, dial it back and run slightly more relaxed until the third cornerstone, then return to a pushed pace to finish the loop. Or run the route as a progressive tempo run, starting at a warm-up pace, building the pace at each cornerstone landmark, and finishing at a 5K race pace. Be mindful that you will have some stoplights and need to cross major intersections along the route. Be ready to pause or stop as needed. Enjoy the breather when the moment arises and have fun exploring Greensboro's urban greenway.

Getting There

There are two designated parking lots to access the Downtown Greenway: 475 Spring Garden St. at Morehead Park (under the colorfully painted concrete bridge) and 750 Plott St. near the Freedom Cornerstone. There is also on-street parking in many places along the loop.

Trail Tip: If you are a first-time trail user, start simple and close to home. Celebrate small victories and drop big expectations. Success comes in many forms. Get out there! Just try it!

Extend Your Trip

Downtown Greensboro has so much to explore and offer visitors in the way of city parks, restaurants, coffee shops, brew pubs, vintage shops, gift shops, art galleries, theater and music performance spaces, museums, and an independent bookstore where you can relax with a glass of wine. Check out downtowngreensboro.org to help plan your adventure. Be on the lookout for special festivals and events throughout the year that you can piggyback onto your Greenway excursion, such as the free NC Folk Festival held every September. There are many adventures awaiting you in Greensboro.

Hungry? Let's Eat!

Joymongers Brewing Co.
576 N. Eugene St., Greensboro, NC 27401
(adjacent to LoFi Park)

"Joymonger," as stated in Urban Dictionary, means "a person who puts on a party, bringing joy to many." Joymongers Brewing Company, started by Greensboro natives, certainly lives up to its name. The open and airy indoor/outdoor space is almost always full with folks relaxing on an afternoon or evening, sampling from the many brews on tap. Often a live band or trivia night will keep things lively. Joymongers doesn't serve food (other than bagged popcorn), but frequently there's a local food truck on-site to please those wanting a little something to accompany their beverages. The

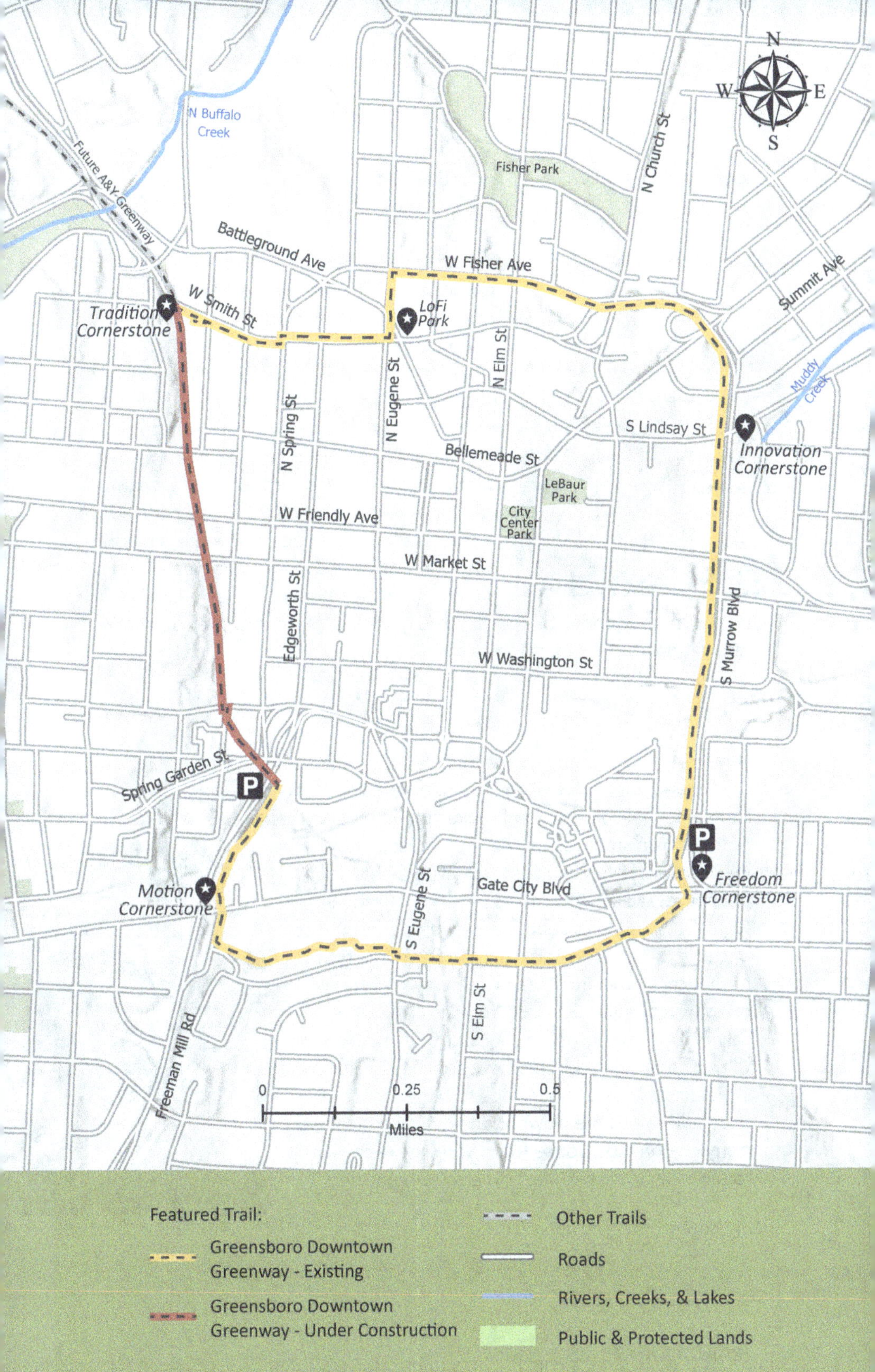
N
W E
S
N Buffalo Creek
Future A&Y Greenway
Battleground Ave
W Fisher Ave
Fisher Park
N Church St
Summit Ave
W Smith St
Tradition Cornerstone
LoFi Park
N Eugene St
N Elm St
S Lindsay St
Muddy Creek
Innovation Cornerstone
N Spring St
Bellemeade St
LeBaur Park
City Center Park
W Friendly Ave
S Murrow Blvd
Edgeworth St
W Market St
W Washington St
Spring Garden St
P
Motion Cornerstone
S Eugene St
Gate City Blvd
P
Freedom Cornerstone
Freeman Mill Rd
S Elm St
0   0.25   0.5
Miles
Featured Trail:
Greensboro Downtown Greenway - Existing
Greensboro Downtown Greenway - Under Construction
Other Trails
Roads
Rivers, Creeks, & Lakes
Public & Protected Lands

taproom is located adjacent to LoFi (Lower Fisher) Park, a sustainably designed space along the Downtown Greenway. Joymongers Barrel Hall, a second location in Winston-Salem, is worth a visit, too.

The Sage Mule
608 Battleground Ave., Greensboro, NC 27401

A downtown favorite for breakfast/brunch/lunch, The Sage Mule serves up a full menu of homemade-from-scratch bakery items, breakfast plates (a hot honey and chicken biscuit, please!), a wide variety of "sammies," burgers and "roughage" (a.k.a. salad) with an incredibly friendly staff to wait on you. They even have daytime cocktails. It's hard to decide what to order, but you truly can't go wrong. The indoor seating is bright and cozy, and there is plentiful outdoor seating under a gazebo or a covered patio. Check their hours before going. They are not open on Monday or Tuesday. It is a popular place, and they don't take reservations, but it's worth the wait.

Cheesecakes by Alex
315 S. Elm St., Greensboro, NC 27401

How often do you find a dessert shop fully dedicated to cheesecake?! Owner and chef/baker Alex Amoroso loves his craft and is very creative and personable. A visit to his bakeshop is a must when in Greensboro. A downtown staple since 2002, Cheesecakes by Alex is one of our clear favorites, with 22 flavors of cheesecake. (Some flavors are even offered in sugar-free, low-sugar, and gluten-free options.) Also available are a full coffee bar, ice cream selections from local Homeland Creamery, many varieties of cakes in very generous slices, cookies, and other bakery items to peruse in the counter windows. With both inside and outside seating along Elm Street, it's a comfortable place to hang out, savor a treat, and watch the downtown goings-on. With so many options to choose from, you may even want to take a little something home to sample later!

PALMER'S TRAIL COOKIES

Who doesn't love a healthy cookie! This versatile cookie recipe will satisfy your hunger on the trail every time. You can swap whole wheat and white flours or use oat bran in place of flax seed meal. Try sunflower seeds in place of pumpkin seeds and any dried fruit. (Palmer's personal favorite is cherries.) Quick cooking oats will result in a softer cookie. For a chewier cookie, slightly under bake the batch, or if you prefer them to be crispier, you can go a minute longer.

DRY INGREDIENTS:

1 cup whole wheat pastry flour
½ cup all-purpose flour
⅓ cup flax seed meal
1 teaspoon ground cinnamon
½ teaspoon baking soda
¼ teaspoon salt

2 cups rolled oats
1 cup semisweet chocolate chips
1 cup dried cherries or cranberries
¾ cup unsweetened shredded coconut
⅓ cup coarsely chopped pumpkin seeds

WET INGREDIENTS:

½ cup unsalted butter, softened
½ cup brown sugar
2 eggs
2 teaspoons vanilla extract

DIRECTIONS:

Preheat oven to 350°F. In a bowl, whisk together the first six dry ingredients. In a separate bowl, beat together softened butter and brown sugar until smooth. With a wooden spoon, stir in eggs and vanilla. Combine flour mixture into the butter mixture. Fold in the oats, chocolate chips, dried fruit, coconut and pumpkin seeds until just combined. Loosely roll into 1 ½ inch balls and place onto the baking sheets about 2 inches apart. Press lightly to flatten slightly. Bake in the preheated oven for about 12 minutes, until lightly golden at the edges. Allow to fully cool before storing in an airtight container.

Guilford County Farm

Distance: **3 miles, lollipop loop**
Difficulty Level: **easy**
Trailhead: **7315 Howerton Rd., or 3220 Amick Rd., Elon, NC 27244**

There's a sunrise and sunset every single day, and they're absolutely free. Don't miss so many of them.
— Jo Walton

Guilford County Farm boasts a mostly easy trail system through a typical Piedmont landscape—varied and rolling, including wide open pasture with beautiful, expansive views, edges of cropland, forests, scenic rock outcroppings, a peaceful pond, and several creek crossings by way of an arched bridge and rock hops. A little-known gem, these trails are perfect for trail runs and easy hikes. Popular with birders because of the diversity of forest and open habitats, the Farm boasts records of 150 different bird species. These trails have been designated part of the NC Mountains-to-Sea Trail and were hand built by volunteers, including signs, benches, and the impressive wooden bridge over the creek in the woods.

If you park at the Howerton Road lot, the trail follows the road for a short distance, then runs along open fields before reaching the forested sections, which provide shade from a wide variety of mature hardwoods and pines. The Amick Road parking area is much smaller but is closer to the quiet pond and forested trails. If you can catch them, sunsets on the Guilford County Farm Trails are magnificent from the open areas.

Be sure to visit the adorable rescue donkeys, Jax and Opie, at the farm pen on Howerton Road.

More to Know

Operating as a prison farm from 1935 to 2015, Guilford County Farm housed inmates who worked the land to learn marketable skills, such as crop maintenance, woodworking, and upholstery, to improve their job prospects after release. Today, this property largely continues to function as agricultural lands in addition to the trail system.

Part of this agricultural system includes a 3-acre vineyard with primarily muscadine varieties, and hosts an annual harvest called The Big Pick on the last weekend of September and the first weekend of October. Volunteers harvest grapes that are distributed throughout the community to local food banks, shelters, and other places that serve those in need. In the spring, the county greenhouse sells annuals and perennials along with vegetable seedlings starting in late March until early May.

Running Thoughts

This 3-mile "course" is ideal for cross country training. One option is to use the first 7–10 minutes as warm-up, then pick up your pace for 3 minutes, return to a steady pace for 2 minutes, repeating 3 minutes on/2 minutes off for the duration of the trail run. Add a 5-minute walk or cool-down jog at the end. If you park at the Amick Road lot, stretching after your run while overlooking the pond can provide a quiet, reflective ending to your workout. Another option is to use the woods (if you parked at Amick Road) or road section (if you parked at Howerton) as your warm-up. Then head up to the grassy space along the fence next to the field. This part of the trail is generally well tended/mowed and rolls along nicely. The straight, grassy path is well suited for running 800s or 1000s. Try 4–6 repeats with a rest between each for a satisfying workout. Keep in mind the grassy field is not shaded, so pick a time of year and/or time of day carefully if choosing the field workout.

Getting There

The large lot on Howerton Road is surrounded by high barbed wire-lined fences left over from its days as a prison farm, but don't worry, you are in the right place, and there are no prisoners on-site. This trailhead offers some picnic tables and a portable restroom. Follow the white circle trail blaze (designating the NC Mountains-to-Sea Trail) down the road and soon you will see the donkey pen where Jax and Opie live. The trail crosses Howerton Road, just past the donkey pen. The smaller Amick Road lot, which is closer to the pond and the forested trails, is also a good starting point.

Extend Your Trip

Elon University, located in the town of Elon, is a short drive from the trail and a beautifully landscaped campus to explore. The word Elon means "oak" in Hebrew. An interactive map online details 125 trees, all different species, on a 1.25-mile walk of campus, which takes approximately 90 minutes to complete. The trees on the trail are marked by plaques that match the numbered map. Visit the campus map tab on the university's website and search for "The Trees of Elon Map." This is an interesting, educational side trip and a nice way to see the campus.

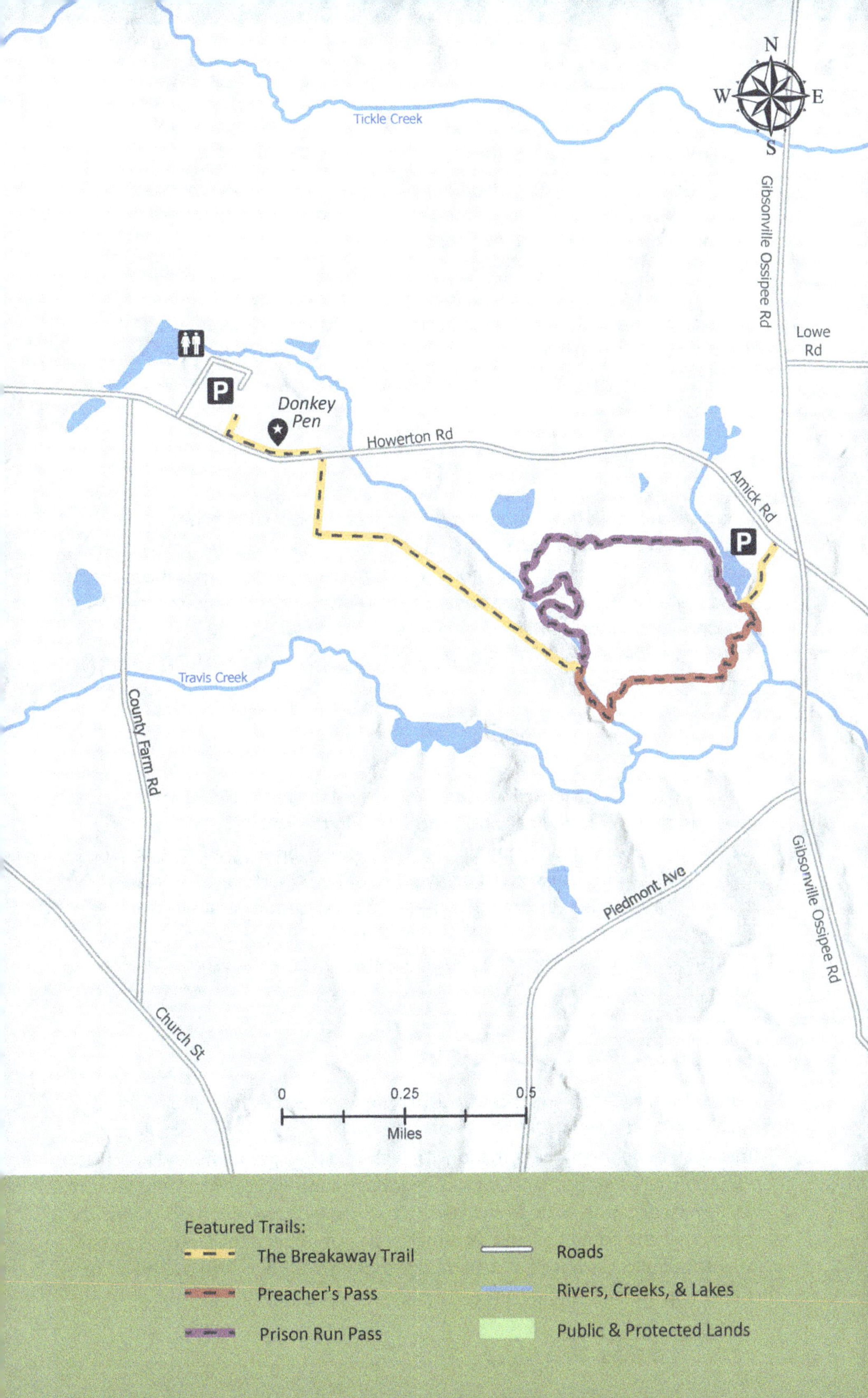

Tickle Creek
N
W E
S
Gibsonville Ossipee Rd
Lowe Rd
P
Donkey Pen
Howerton Rd
Amick Rd
P
Travis Creek
County Farm Rd
Piedmont Ave
Gibsonville Ossipee Rd
Church St
0   0.25   0.5
Miles
Featured Trails:
The Breakaway Trail
Preacher's Pass
Prison Run Pass
Roads
Rivers, Creeks, & Lakes
Public & Protected Lands

Hungry? Let's Eat!

Downtown Gibsonville is a stone's throw from the trailhead and has some delicious options for treats after your farm adventure. A sizable park runs along the railroad tracks right in the middle of town, making it a great space to enjoy tasty take-out treats. Trains are a big part of Gibsonville's history. If you wander through the park on a Saturday morning, you might see the outdoor Gibsonville Garden Railroad in action, with over 2,400 feet of train track and 20 model trains running at one time. Created in 1996 by a retired freight conductor on the Southern Railroad, the model details some of the history of Gibsonville and other featured historic moments and places in North Carolina.

Maple View's County Line Creamery Company
113 E. Main St., Gibsonville, NC 27249

Located on Main Street, this adorable ice cream shop, with its black-and-white checkered floor and decor, is a cool treat on a warm day. Maple View ice cream touts "from farm to cone" and is made with locally produced whole cow's milk, free of added hormones or antibiotics. They have won local, regional, and national awards for their products. Stop in and try one of their many flavors in a cone or cup, or try a shake or a banana split. Maple View is sure to please all ages.

Toasty Kettlyst Beer Company
106 W. Main St., Gibsonville, NC 27249

This husband-and-wife-owned brewery was established in 2020. It's a great find and part of the revitalization happening in this small town. They offer beers brewed on-site in many different varieties. Come try a flight or dive right in with a pint or two, and pair your beer with music or trivia. (Check their Facebook page for the schedule and hours.) Seating is available out back on the patio or inside the tasting room. If you are hungry, bring in a pizza or other snack from down the street. Several nearby establishments offer take-out food options.

Once Upon A Chocolate
139 Piedmont Ave., Gibsonville, NC 27249

Once Upon a Chocolate, located just around the corner from Main Street, is a sweet find. Owner Debbie Stephens is welcoming and personable and makes all her chocolates by hand with high-quality ingredients and no preservatives. There are thousands of molded shapes and designs for every season and every occasion. Stop in and peruse the many displays, and don't miss the options at the counter. A mix-and-match box of chocolates is always a good way to sample. Go ahead, you earned it today after your farm trail adventure! Closed on Sunday.

Cane Creek Mountains Natural Area

Distance: **up to 9.4 miles, multiple loops**
Difficulty Level: **moderate**
Trailhead: **5075 Bass Mountain Rd. (Pine Hill Trailhead), or 5545 Bass Mountain Rd. (Oak Hill Trailhead), Snow Camp, NC 27349**

Adopt the pace of nature: her secret is patience.
— Ralph Waldo Emerson

With close proximity to both the Triad and Triangle, Cane Creek Mountains Natural Area in southern Alamance County offers a variety of trails and experiences at two different trailheads. The Pine Hill Trailhead provides access to the 2.5-mile Northern Approach Trail and the 1-mile Longleaf Loop. The Northern Approach Trail climbs up one of the highest mountain peaks east of Greensboro (987-foot elevation), offering a good workout while winding past interesting rock formations, rocky streams, and views at the top, particularly during winter months when leaves are off the trees. The Longleaf Loop meanders through recently planted longleaf pine forests and wetland areas abundant with birds. It is relatively flat, with winding boardwalks, making it a great trail for beginner trail runners, jogger strollers, or people seeking less of a challenge. At the Oak Hill Trailhead, there are two new trails: the 3.4-mile Pioneer Camp Trail and the 2.5-mile Lookout Trail. The Pioneer Camp Trail winds through a quiet forest with several stream crossings, passing remnants of the Pioneer Youth Camp, including a stone chimney and cabins, which operated in the summers from 1937 to 1956. The Lookout Trail is designed for families and new trail users, with relatively gentle slopes. A future observation tower is planned where this trail meets the Northern Approach Trail at the top.

The trails are color-coded and well-marked with matching blazes every tenth of a mile. A four-digit code on each blaze is designed to help park staff or emergency responders locate you if needed. The park totals over 1,000 acres and includes camping facilities. Parking at either trailhead provides access to the entire trail network. Additional trails are planned for the future.

More to Know

The Cane Creek Mountains are part of a small, ancient mountain chain, eroded remnants of once sizable peaks. Because of the elevation and rugged nature of these mountains, there are many species that are not found frequently in Alamance County or elsewhere in the Piedmont region. Keep an eye out for the eight types of ferns found here and wild blueberries.

Running Thoughts

The Northern Approach, Pioneer Camp, and Lookout Trails are primarily single track. Some sections climb and wind and are extremely rocky. Your pace will probably slow significantly in these sections of the trails, but they are a great workout, both for your cardio and muscular systems. These loops range in their level of challenge, so pick a pace that fits your ability. If you are an experienced trail runner and are looking for a place to train for the Uwharrie Mountain Runs or a run or event using technical footwork, these trails are a great find. Want a flatter, easier run, or thinking about mile repeats on a soft surface? Give the Longleaf Loop a try. It's not shaded like the other trails, so keep in mind the season and weather when choosing this loop.

Getting There

There are currently two parking areas to access the trail networks, both located south of Burlington off NC Hwy. 87 on Bass Mountain Road and clearly marked with large, attractive signs. The Pine Hill Trailhead parking lot is at the end of a 0.25-mile winding gravel entrance road. The Oak Hill Trailhead parking area is located less than 1 mile south on Bass Mountain Road from the Pine Hill Trailhead. Both parking areas have pit restrooms.

Extend Your Trip

Close by is Cedarock Park, a 500-acre nature park managed by Alamance County. The park includes 6 miles of hiking trails and 6 miles of equestrian trails. The hiking trails are mostly shaded with some boardwalks, bridges, and creek access. There are also two disc golf courses, a footgolf course, a restored late-1800s historical farm with resident farm animals, two fishing ponds, a picturesque waterfall over an old mill dam, picnic shelters and gazebos, basketball court, volleyball court, playground, canoe and kayak rentals, camping, and ample field space for open play. With something for everyone at the park, you can easily spend a day in this part of the region.

Trail Tip: *Focus on form in the second half of your hike or run. Pick up your feet and knees. There can be a tendency to trip or fall on uneven trail surfaces when you get tired.*

Hungry? Let's Eat!

Consider a visit to the City of Burlington, only a short drive from the Cane Creek Mountains Natural Area. It's a great place to end your day's adventure.

City Park and Amusement Area
1388 Main St., Burlington, NC 27215
Bring a picnic lunch and visit Burlington's City Park with its recently restored carousel and new building to house it. The historic Dentzel Menagerie Carousel, built around 1906–1910 and purchased by the City of Burlington in

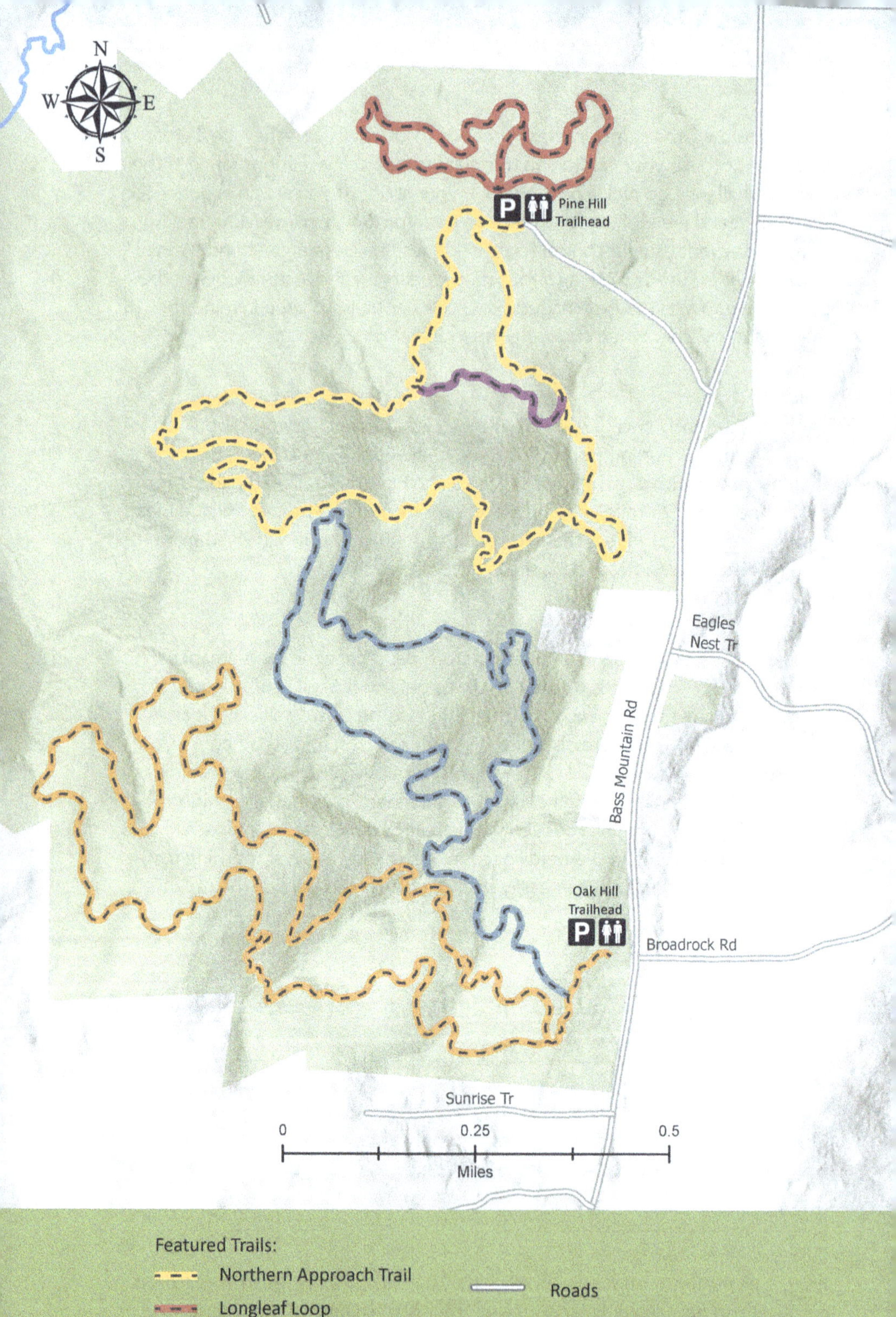

N
W
E
S
Pine Hill
Trailhead
P
Eagles
Nest Tr
Bass Mountain Rd
Oak Hill
Trailhead
P
Broadrock Rd
Sunrise Tr
0
0.25
0.5
Miles
Featured Trails:
Northern Approach Trail
Longleaf Loop
Heartland Loop
Lookout Trail
Pioneer Camp Trail
Roads
Rivers, Creeks, & Lakes
Public & Protected Lands

1948, features 48 wooden hand-carved animals. Operating year-round and with a modest price to ride, it is fun for kids and adults alike. Check ride times online. It is open only on weekends during the winter months. The park has other small amusement rides and a train. City Park is home to ball fields and many other sports facilities owned and managed by the city. Picnic tables and shelters are available, as well as a walking track and trail. A lovely stream winds through the park.

Smitty's Ice Cream
107 E. Front St., Burlington, NC 27215
Smitty's makes small-batch, handcrafted, premium ice cream with as many locally sourced, seasonal ingredients as possible. The shop offers customers a wide variety of flavors to choose from, including your favorite standards as well as unique seasonal creations and dairy-free/vegan options. (We should mention, too, that the homemade waffle cones have spectacular flavor and crunch.) The shop has plenty of outdoor seating and indoor options with windows open in nice weather. Feel free to pull a game or book off the shelf and stay awhile. You might find yourself visiting again and again. This small business has three locations: the Burlington shop, another in Graham, and a third in Elon, all delicious choices for sweet treats.

Another great option to explore and a short drive from the trailhead is the revitalized and artistic downtown of Graham, with its soda shops, lunch spots, and colorful murals decorating city spaces. There are many options for satisfying your hunger in town, but Press won our hearts (and tummies).

Press Coffee+Crepes
133 N. Main St., Graham, NC 27253
Located on Main Street, this old-world European coffee and crepes shop has mouthwatering options for a post-trail experience. Press offers customers many delicious savory and sweet options for breakfast and lunch, including breakfast crepes, salads, and sandwiches, as well as weekday and weekend specials. Be sure to check out the local artists' works on the walls, which rotate quarterly and are for sale. Indoor

and umbrella/patio tables are available for dining in. Orders can also be placed online for pickup. If you live in the Triangle, check out Press' second location on Blackwell Street in Durham.

GORP

Trail mix often goes by the acronym GORP, but what does it stand for? It is said that GORP is either "good old raisins and peanuts" or "granola, oats, raisins, peanuts." Its origin is actually a bit unclear, too, with references as far back as Danish students in 1833 describing GORP-like mixtures. In the mid-1900s trail mix was mainly raisins and nuts, giving trail goers some natural sugar, fat, and protein. The *Oxford English Dictionary* cites a 1913 reference to the verb gorp meaning "to eat greedily," so perhaps it is a backronym. Whichever is correct, mix your own and find your favorite sweet and salty combination to take with you on your next trail adventure. Change it up every time or stick to your favorite combo!

INGREDIENTS:

raisins
dried cranberries
dried cherries
peanuts
almonds
pecans
cashews
pistachios
sunflower or pumpkin seeds
granola
chocolate chips
candy-coated chocolates
chocolate-coated nuts/fruits
toasted coconut flakes

DIRECTIONS:

In a small bowl or plastic bag, add ¼ cup of three or more of your favorite ingredients, choosing from a selection of nuts, seeds, fruits, and chocolate. The options are vast. Mix and enjoy!

Note: if you add chocolate to your GORP in the warmer months, make sure it's candy coated. Chocolate without the coating does not hold up well in the heat. (Melted chocolate, nut, and fruit clusters are tasty, but very messy!)

Crow Branch Overlook Trail, Carolina North Forest

Distance: **4.2 miles, loop**

Difficulty Level: **easy**

Trailhead: **end of Municipal Dr., Chapel Hill, NC 27516**

A walk in nature walks the soul back home.
— Mary Davis

With 750 acres of woods, Carolina North Forest is a true respite from the busy and highly urbanized surrounding areas of Chapel Hill and Carrboro. Home to a large network of trails, Carolina North Forest can be a little tricky to navigate at first, but the Crow Branch Overlook Trail is a well-marked, single-track loop trail for the novice hiker/runner that can help you get oriented to the forest. Follow the numbered blazes and you will easily stay on track.

With rolling terrain through a mostly pine forest with some hardwoods, interesting rock outcrops, and a scenic lake with benches for a rest or simply quiet reflection, the Crow Branch Overlook Trail is a local favorite. If you live close by, you will come back again and again. Every season has something to offer, with bright green ferns and mosses in the spring, cool shade in the summer, impressive color in the fall, and clear views in the winter. Crow Branch is open to mountain bikers, so keep an eye out. The trails are typically closed after rain. Check their website for updates.

More to Know

Carolina North Forest, sometimes referred to as the Horace Williams Tract, was donated to UNC-Chapel Hill in 1940 by Horace Williams. Williams earned the university's first advanced degree and was its first professor of philosophy. UNC-Chapel Hill has considered plans for developing the south-eastern sections of the property around the former Horace Williams Airport, while preserving the majority of the property for low-impact recreational use.

Running Thoughts

This is one of Hollis' favorite single-track running trails, with lots of pine straw for soft cushioning underfoot and plentiful shade with beautiful filtered light through the trees. Make it a solo, untimed run, or invite a friend to talk and run for some easy miles. Feel like racing it? Check out the annual Philosopher's Way Trail Runs held each spring, with distances of either 7K or 10 miles.

Trail Tip: Hiking with a companion (person or pet) as a shared experience is safer and can be more fun. If solo, let someone know of your trail plans.

Getting There

Parking is located at the end of Municipal Drive, approximately 0.5 miles from Martin Luther King Boulevard. This gravel lot has a couple of portable toilets, should you need a restroom. After parking, enter through the gate and follow the gravel road, known as Pumpkin Loop Trail, for less than 0.25 miles until you see the Crow Branch Overlook Trail signpost on the right-hand side. Angle to the right and follow the round, green numbering system counter-clockwise on the loop.

Extend Your Trip

If you are looking to extend your stay within Carolina North Forest, consider adding the wider 2.5-mile Pumpkin Loop, which circles around the Crow Branch Overlook Trail. It is popular for mountain biking and running (perfect for novice trail runners), or there are many more miles of other single-track trails in Carolina North Forest.

For a "don't miss" experience and fantastic educational opportunity, consider a visit to the North Carolina Botanical Garden, located only 4 miles away just outside of the UNC-Chapel Hill campus. Free to the public, the garden offers delightful walks through 15 different themed display gardens showcasing the diversity of plants from all areas of North Carolina. The taste-fully and sustainably designed Allen Education Center features an art gallery, exhibit hall, a discovery room for children, and a garden shop with a variety of botanical-themed books, local art, gifts, and even seeds and native plants for your nature-loving friends and family. No pets are allowed in the Botanical Garden. Although the Garden is closed on Monday, their 3-mile network of Piedmont Nature Trails located outside of the Garden gates is open every day, dawn to dusk, and welcomes pets on leash.

Hungry? Let's Eat!

Carolina Coffee Shop
138 E. Franklin St., Chapel Hill, NC 27514

Serving Tar Heels for over a century, Carolina Coffee Shop is the oldest continually running restaurant in the state. They are still locally owned and operated, serving breakfast, brunch, lunch, coffee, and cocktails. There are

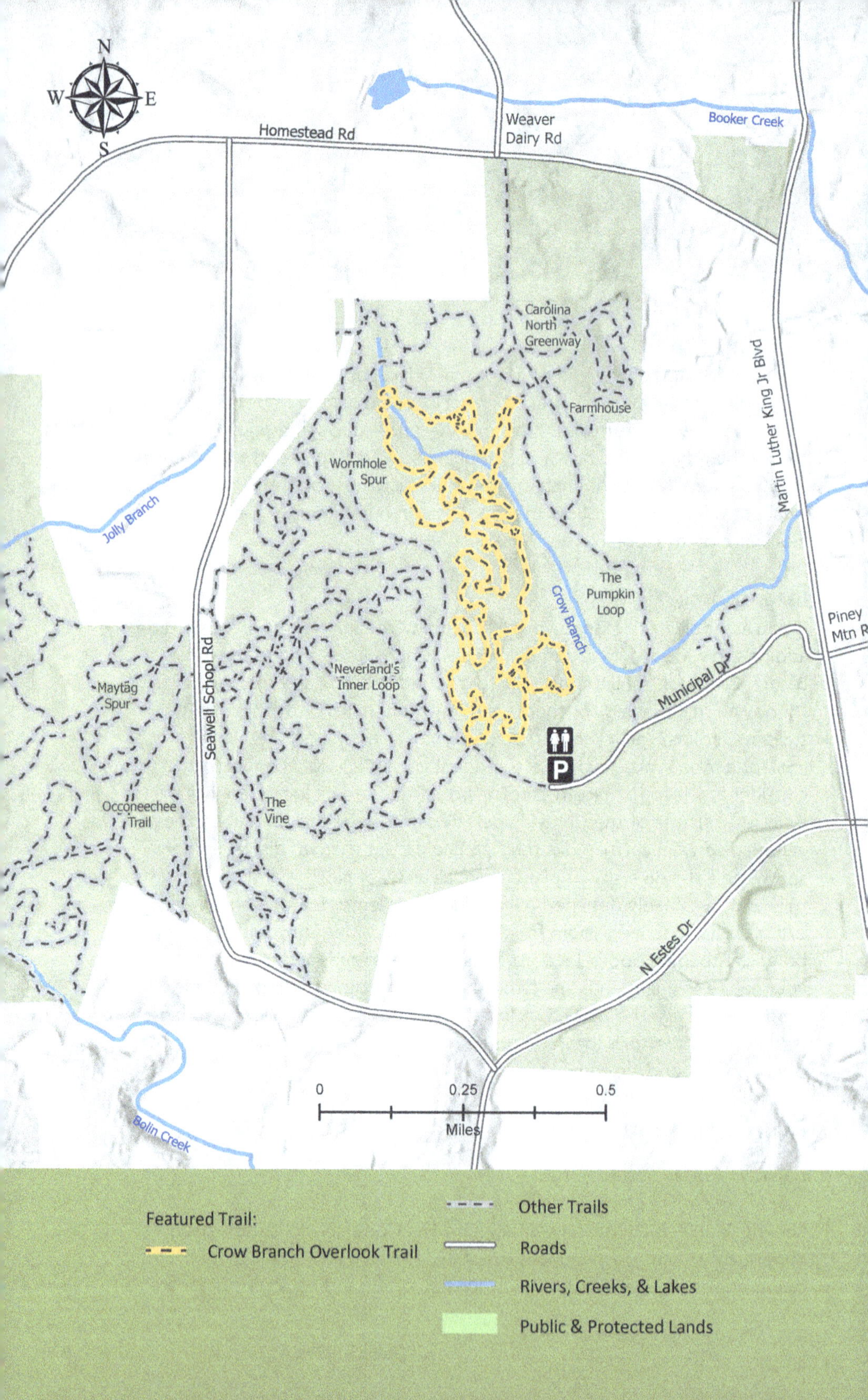

N
W E
S
Homestead Rd
Weaver Dairy Rd
Booker Creek
Carolina North Greenway
Farmhouse
Martin Luther King Jr Blvd
Wormhole Spur
Jolly Branch
Crow Branch
The Pumpkin Loop
Piney Mtn Rd
Seawell School Rd
Neverland's Inner Loop
Municipal Dr
Maytag Spur
Occoneechee Trail
The Vine
N Estes Dr
Bolin Creek
0   0.25   0.5
Miles
Featured Trail:
Crow Branch Overlook Trail
Other Trails
Roads
Rivers, Creeks, & Lakes
Public & Protected Lands

many delicious options here to curb your appetite or quench your thirst after your trail adventure. In good weather, the outdoor street-side patio on Franklin Street is a lively dining experience. Or choose indoor seating options, with comfortable tables and private booths surrounded by old café charm with wood floors and exposed brick walls. It's a popular spot for many UNC-Chapel Hill professors, students, and alumni, as well as locals and visitors to town.

The Yogurt Pump (YoPo)
106 W. Franklin St., Chapel Hill, NC 27516

Labeled "the place to Chill on the Hill" and better known as "YoPo" to students and locals, The Yogurt Pump has been serving delicious frozen yogurt creations since 1982, when the concept was brand new. The Yogurt Pump was the first frozen yogurt shop in the state of North Carolina. High-quality frozen yogurt and service with a smile from the "YoPros" make this a treasured Chapel Hill institution. When you enter the shop, tucked into its alcove on Franklin Street, you'll be greeted by sweet smells and have many amazing 
flavors to choose from, which rotate daily. With selections of crispy waffle, cake cone, or cup, and many toppings, the combinations are endless! It's a sweet way to conclude your day's adventure.

Mediterranean Deli, Bakery, and Catering
410 W. Franklin St., Chapel Hill, NC 27516

Operating since 1992, this family-owned restaurant features fresh, locally sourced, authentic Mediterranean and Middle Eastern foods. The deli case, with over 60 items to choose from, offers mouthwatering salads, spreads, hot entrées, and freshly made bakery items. It is a feast for your eyes, and you might have a hard time deciding what to order. A few years back, a Jordanian friend who was visiting Hollis' family declared, "It's perfect." Many of the offerings are vegan and gluten-free. Med Deli makes all of their own pita bread on-site, and sometimes you can see the hot, puffy pita bread as it cools on racks. Take-out or eat-in are both options. Indoor tables and outdoor street-side patio tables are available. Closed on Sunday.

Mediterranean Deli had a devastating fire as we were writing *Trails & Treats*. They are rebuilding in the old location but currently are offering online take-out orders from 425 W. Franklin St. Be patient and support them during the rebuilding process. We simply could not leave them out of the book! They are a Chapel Hill staple.

Johnston Mill
Nature Preserve

Distance: **4.6 miles, multiple loops**

Difficulty Level: **easy**

Trailhead: **2713 Mt. Sinai Rd., or 6001 Turkey Farm Rd., Chapel Hill, NC 27514**

In nature, nothing is perfect and everything is perfect. Trees can be contorted, bent in weird ways, and they're still beautiful.
— Alice Walker

riangle Land Conservancy's 296-acre Johnston Mill Nature Preserve is one of our favorite spots in the Triangle. It offers 4.6 miles of quiet trails to walk or run and is much less crowded than the more popular nearby Eno River State Park and Duke Forest trails.

The varied terrain at Johnston Mill Preserve includes the Robin's Branch Trail, which follows a scenic rocky and placid section of New Hope Creek; the Beech Loop Trail, with its steep bluffs and impressive stands of mature beech trees, some as old as 150 years; and the Old Field Bluff Trail, which passes through an early successional forest. Aphid Alley is a wooded connector, and the Bluebird Trail follows a powerline easement, so it is exposed to the sun and can be hot in warm weather.

Look for some interesting landmarks on these well-marked trails, including fascinating tree and root shapes, and creative bridges and benches with memorial plaques. The spring wildflowers are spectacular. This is an ideal trail for kids to enjoy nature: there are ample places to access the creek, climb on rocks, listen for frogs, or spot one of the many species of birds.

More to Know

Johnston Mill Preserve is named for the Johnston family, who farmed this property and ran two grist mills along New Hope Creek beginning in the 1700s for 200 years. During winter months you may see vestiges of the Johnston family's farm, including crumbling stone chimneys and grist mill remnants.

New Hope Creek, which drains into Jordan Lake, is one of the largest areas of contiguous preserved open spaces in the region. Johnston Mill Preserve is one of many protected tracts within the watershed providing benefits for drinking water supplies and wildlife habitats.

Running Thoughts

These trail loops are great for running any time of year. Try a workout running with a partner, taking turns as to who is leading. Every 10 minutes, trade off the lead, and let the front runner determine the pace and the route. The miles will go by quickly, so don't forget to look around and take in the beauty of the preserve as you run.

Getting There

There are two parking lots to access Johnston Mill Preserve, one on Mount Sinai Road and the other on Turkey Farm Road. Both lots often fill up on weekends, so arrive early or go during the week.

Extend Your Trip

Nearby Duke Forest offers an extensive network of trails open to the public. Consider trying the Rhododendron Bluff circuit trails (with rock scrambles) along New Hope Creek. The trailhead parking is located off Whitfield Road. Note: sometimes Duke Forest trails are closed for management activities, typically from September through December. Check dukeforest.duke.edu for trail updates and information before going.

Hungry? Let's Eat!

The Pig
630 Weaver Dairy Rd., #101, Chapel Hill, NC 27514

The Pig is tended by owner and chef Sam Suchoff. His passion for cooking is displayed with a very diverse menu that features barbecue made from local, pasture-raised, antibiotic- and hormone-free pork. Other delicious options include Shiitake tacos, catfish po-boy and BBQ tempeh sandwiches, gumbo, and beef brisket. There are also many flavorful Southern sides to choose from, such as collard greens, mac and cheese, beer-baked beans, and a not-to-miss item, the homemade pickles. Indoor and outdoor seating is available. A little bookshelf near the front counter gives you some cookbook and other local book options to check out while you wait for your order. Maybe *Trails & Treats* will make it onto the shelf! Closed on Sunday.

Joe Van Gogh
1129 Weaver Dairy Rd., Ste. AD, Chapel Hill, NC 27514

Located in Timberlyne Shopping Center, next to the Chelsea Theater (one of the best art and independent film theaters in the Triangle), Joe Van Gogh will inspire you with an artful coffee experience. On their menu are latte, mocha, chai, and many more specialty coffee drinks. "We take pride in the art and craft of everything we do from seed to service and from concept to cup." To accompany your "cup of joe," made-from-scratch, responsibly sourced breakfast and lunch items are prepared fresh daily, including savory and sweet pastries, breakfast biscuits, and sandwiches. If you are short on time or want

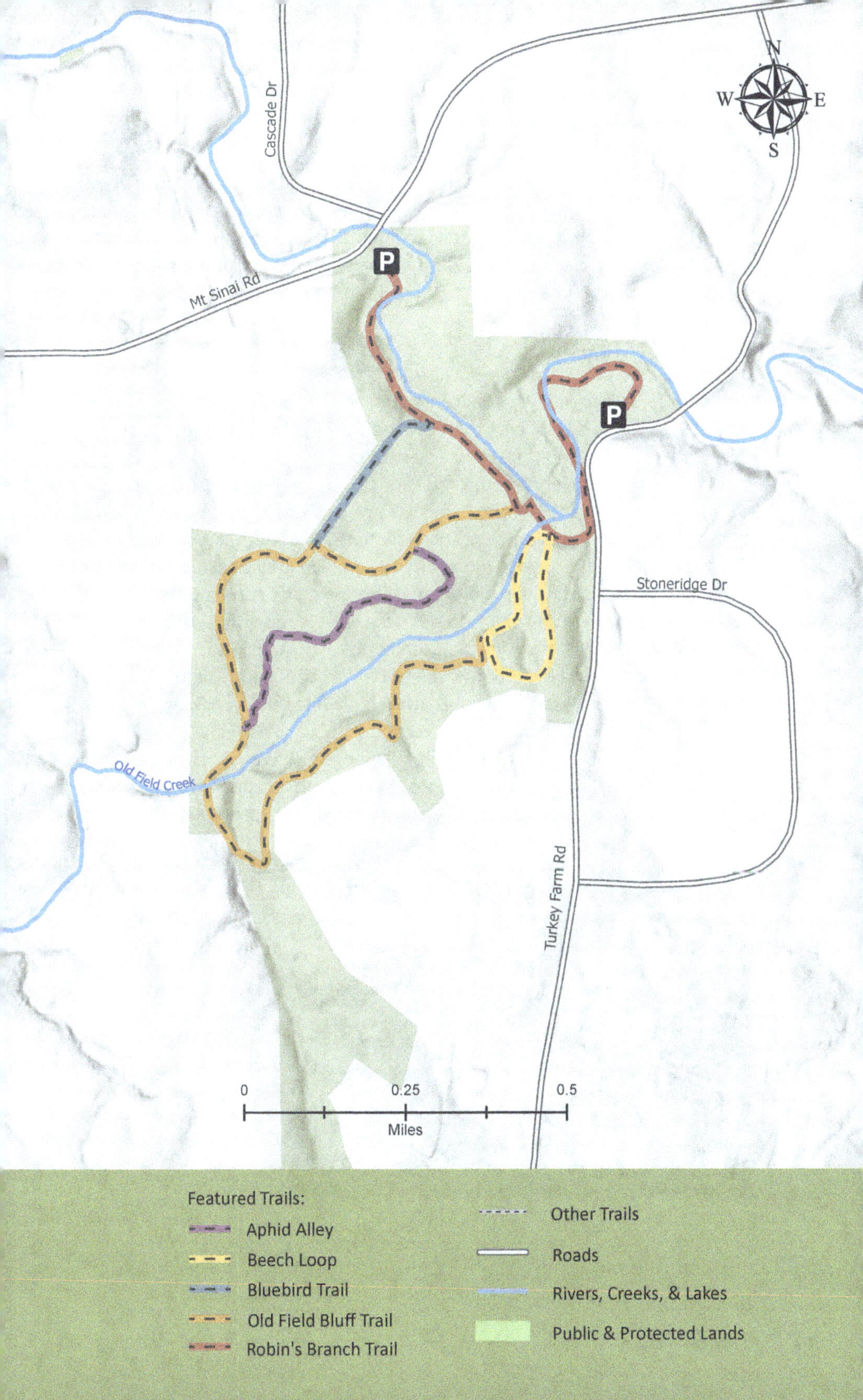

N
W E
S
Cascade Dr
Mt Sinai Rd
P
P
Stoneridge Dr
Old Field Creek
Turkey Farm Rd
0
0.25
0.5
Miles
Featured Trails:
Aphid Alley
Beech Loop
Bluebird Trail
Old Field Bluff Trail
Robin's Branch Trail
Other Trails
Roads
Rivers, Creeks, & Lakes
Public & Protected Lands

it ready for pickup, an online option is available to place your order ahead of arriving. If you plan to stay and be leisurely, indoor and outside café tables await you. Additional café locations can be found in Durham and Raleigh, all with the same high-quality standards and care for our Earth through environmental, social, and economic sustainability practices. Joe Van Gogh supports many North Carolina nonprofits. One of their community partners is Friends of the Mountains-to-Sea Trail.

Carrburritos
711 W. Rosemary St., Carrboro, NC 27510

This unique California-style Mexican restaurant has been around for over 25 years and serves up one of the best and freshest burritos in the Triangle. With many filling options (pork, chicken, beef, fish, and several vegetarian options), you will never run out of versions to try on return visits. If you decide you don't want a burrito, they also offer tacos, tostadas, and quesadillas, as well as appetizers and side items. Order at the counter and they will bring it to your table, or you can take it to go. Chips, which accompany most orders, are a mixture of house-made corn and flour tortillas, and are out-of-this-world delicious! A selection of six different homemade salsas will keep your mouth happy, from a mild salsa fresca to a spicy habanero, and everything in between. To cool your palate, give their horchata a try. Beer, margaritas, and other beverage selections can round out your order. Colorful oilcloths cover the indoor tables, while a small gated garden patio space with beautiful plantings makes another great seating option. If you are in Davidson, stop into their second location on Main Street. Both locations are closed on Sunday and Monday. Buen provecho!

Relax for lunch or dinner on Carrburritos' patio.

18 Occoneechee Speedway Trail

Distance: **4 miles, lollipop loop**
Difficulty Level: **easy**
Trailhead: **320 Elizabeth Brady Rd., Hillsborough, NC 27278**

*To me a lush carpet of pine needles or spongy grass
is more welcome than the most luxurious Persian rug.*
— Helen Keller

Occoneechee Speedway may not sound like a place to hike or trail run, but it is one of the most interesting and unique trails in the Triangle. You don't want to miss this one!

One of only three racetracks in the country listed on the National Register of Historic Places, the Speedway sits on 44 acres on the banks of the Eno River and is the only surviving dirt speedway from NASCAR's inaugural season in 1949. The oval track attracted the best stock car racers until it shut down in 1968. Today the Speedway celebrates this history with artifacts from its heyday, including broken-down cars and the original grandstands, reminding visitors of its former era as one of NASCAR's premier tracks.

Occoneechee Speedway has 4 miles of trails, including the Speedway Trace, the Spectator Trace loop that runs above the track, and others. The Occoneechee Speedway Trail is part of the NC Mountains-to-Sea Trail. Imagine hurtling around the racetrack with no guardrails and the threat of ending up in the Eno River!

More to Know

As you walk or run on the soft pine straw on these now shaded paths, you will follow in the tracks of many NASCAR early legends, including Fireball Roberts, Richard Petty, Junior Johnson, and Louise Smith (NASCAR's first female driver). Imagine the large cheering crowds of up to 15,000 people in

the grandstands on Sundays! Allegedly, the Orange County Anti-Racing Association, which formed due to lack of attendance in local churches, managed to permanently close the track in September 1968. A young Richard Petty won the last race ever run there, ending a nearly 20-year tradition.

The Speedway is named for the Native American Occoneechee Band (Occaneechi) of the Saponi Nation, who lived and roamed along the Eno River in what is now Hillsborough and remained there until the early 1700s.

Trail Tip: *Consider your fitness level. If you are new to trails, start slowly to ensure a pleasurable experience and pick a trail under 5 miles with minimal climbing.*

Running Thoughts

Warm up on the perimeter trails leading to the track and enjoy the tranquility of the woods. If you like to do form drills, the track straightaway is ideal for this, and then go into a simple track workout of repeat laps (1000 meters). The oval track's wide, soft, shaded surface is a joy to run. Time one lap, give yourself a minute or two to recover, and try to run the next lap in the same time, repeating for five laps, aiming to keep your times consistent. (1000 x 5 is equal to a 5K or 3.1 miles of speedwork.) Another good workout here is to run the old stadium steps. Steady pace up and jog or walk down, then repeat. If you like unique races, check out the Occoneechee Speedway Relay. It is a 20-lap race held every January on the forested oval. You can choose to run as a two- or four-person team, dividing laps among the teammates. Racers, start your engines!

Getting There

Located just off I-85, there is parking at the trailhead in a gravel lot off Elizabeth Brady Road and some overflow parking along the road if the lot is full. If restrooms are required before you hike, we recommend a stop in downtown Hillsborough. Parking is free in the public parking deck behind Weaver Street Market. You can start here and incorporate the Riverwalk into your walk or run. The 2 miles of greenway, noted below in Extend Your Trip, is a nice addition to your day.

Extend Your Trip

Directly across the road from the trailhead parking lot is the start of Hillsborough's Riverwalk, a paved greenway along the Eno River that stretches nearly 2 miles from Occoneechee Speedway to Hillsborough's historic downtown, passing the Vietri Outlet, Hillsborough Urban Gardens, the historic Occaneechi Village Replica Site, River Park, and the Eno River Farmers Market (open year-round on Saturday) along the way. The Riverwalk is part of the NC Mountains-to-Sea Trail, which you can continue to follow past Occoneechee, heading east for another 1.5 miles toward US Hwy. 70.

Alternatively, travel a short 2.6 miles down the road to reach the Occoneechee Mountain State Natural Area, where a short hike up the mountain will reward you with scenic views from the top of the highest point in Orange County. This special place is protected as a State Natural Area because it hosts a relatively undisturbed diversity of plants and wildlife, including many species found more commonly in the mountains such as mountain laurel and rhododendron. There is a significantly large population of the brown elfin butterfly, which is believed to have persisted at Occoneechee

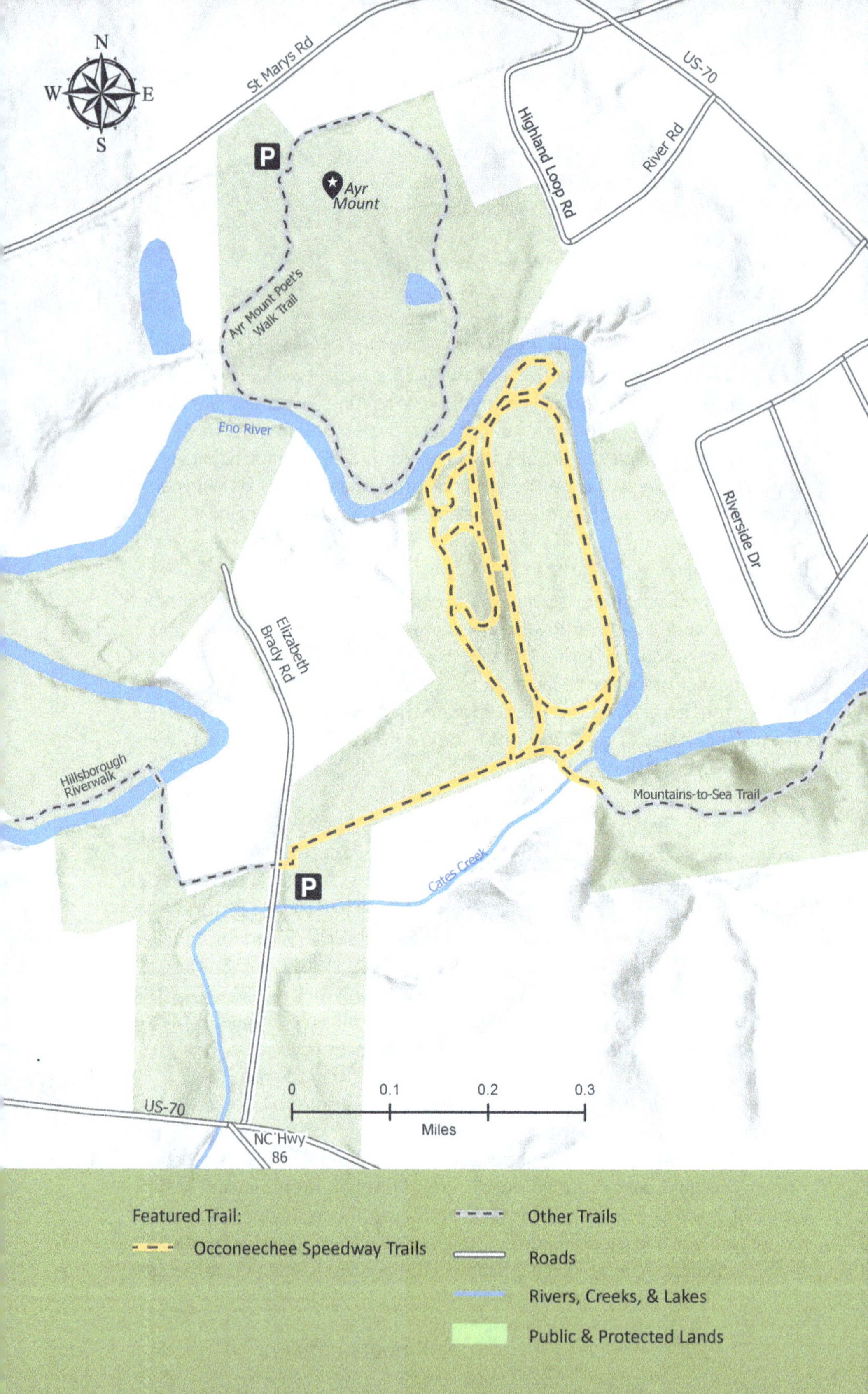

N
W
E
S
St Marys Rd
US-70
Highland Loop Rd
River Rd
P
Ayr Mount
Ayr Mount Poet's Walk Trail
Riverside Dr
Eno River
Elizabeth Brady Rd
Hillsborough Riverwalk
Mountains-to-Sea Trail
Cates Creek
P
US-70
NC Hwy 86
0
0.1
0.2
0.3
Miles
Featured Trail:
Occoneechee Speedway Trails
Other Trails
Roads
Rivers, Creeks, & Lakes
Public & Protected Lands

Mountain since the Ice Age and is found virtually nowhere else in the Piedmont. Explore the 3 miles of trails here to experience the river as well as the mountaintop.

You can also try the 1-mile Poet's Walk at Ayr Mount, located only 2.4 miles away. The trail is open to the public free of charge. Built in 1815, the historic home is open for guided tours for a fee, April through November.

Hungry? Let's Eat!

Hillsborough, the county seat in Orange County, has a quaint, historic downtown, and is located just a few minutes' drive from the trailhead. There are many great options for a treat in Hillsborough. Some delicious choices (that don't mind sweaty bodies) include Hillsborough BBQ, Radius Pizzeria and Pub, The Wooden Nickel, Los Altos Restaurant, and El Restaurante Ixtapa. All of these are locally owned, offer outdoor seating, and will tempt your taste buds with delicious flavors. One place that gets special mention in this chapter is Weaver Street Market. It is the reason this book exists. Their oatmeal raisin cookies, apple pie, cinnamon rolls, and breads were the inspiration for pairing delicious treats and trails together in a guidebook. Thank you, Weaver Street! For more information about these and other restaurants, check out visithillsboroughnc.com. You can also find details online about festivals and special events in town that might be fun to piggyback onto your trail adventure.

Weaver Street Market
228 S. Churton St., Hillsborough, NC 27278
Weaver Street Market is a co-op, meaning "by the community," and is owned by its employees and members. Their mission—making healthy food more accessible, supporting local agriculture, building community, and protecting the environment—is consistent throughout all four co-op locations in the Triangle. Everything they stock at Weaver Street Market is fresh, healthy, and  sustainable. This special place is full of local produce; delicious prepared foods, including a salad and hot bar; and carefully selected shelf items. But most of all, it is home to some of the best baked goods in the state. Cookies or a slice of pie from Weaver Street Market are a heavenly treat to enjoy on the patio in front of the store. It's a delicious way to relax after a walk or workout in the woods. It's all so good, you'll want to take a little something home for later.

Cox Mountain Trail, Eno River State Park

Distance: **4.1 miles, lollipop loop**
Difficulty Level: **moderate**
Trailhead: **Fews Ford Access, 6101 Cole Mill Rd., Durham, NC 27705**

Nature is one of the most underutilized treasures in life. It has the power to unburden hearts and reconnect to that inner place of peace.
— Dr. Janice Anderson & Kiersten Anderson

Cox Mountain Trail is one of the longer trails in Eno River State Park, beginning in the Fews Ford picnic area and following circular, blue blazes. This 4.1-mile trail starts by taking you down to the river, where you'll cross an impressive, narrow suspension bridge over the water. As you approach the bridge, take note of the signage height and the mention of where the water rose during Hurricane Fran in 1996. Hopefully the water level the day you visit is well below it!

We suggest following the Cox Mountain Trail in a clockwise direction (take the left option), climbing Cox Mountain first, then meandering back down toward the river on the north side. The trail wiggles along the Eno, where you might spot birds, turtles, snakes, and other wildlife, and hear the soothing sounds of flowing waters. Beautiful views along this part of the trail make it a lovely spot for reflection, possibly finding a resting place on some of the large river rocks. In the springtime, moss, ferns, bluets, and other wild-flowers grace the water's edge. You can choose to detour onto the Fanny's Ford Trail, extending your route along the river, or continue on the Cox Mountain Trail, where the shady forest path is sprinkled with mountain laurel blooming in the spring and plentiful ferns. Both routes will take you back to the bridge. Close to the bridge, you will find a short spur trail leading to a historic cabin that is interesting for kids to explore. Once ready, retrace your steps to the picnic and parking area.

Note: low areas on the trail can be very muddy after a rain.

More to Know

The Eno River was once threatened with damming to create a water supply for the City of Durham. Forward-thinking citizens successfully lobbied for the creation of a state park along the river to protect its free-flowing waters. Today, the Eno River State Park extends 13 miles along the river and covers 4,319 acres straddling Durham and Orange Counties. Between the five access points, there are approximately 31 miles of trails and many pristine views of the Eno. It's a reliable destination any time of year for hikers and runners. The prohibition on bicycles makes these trails desirable for those exploring on foot.

Running Thoughts

With terrain changes throughout, this trail should be considered moderately strenuous for running and is a good challenge for runners of any level. There is a 270-foot elevation gain on the trail, offering a hill workout up Cox Mountain and plenty of technical footwork with roots to navigate, especially along the river. Almost completely shaded, Cox Mountain Trail offers superb sections where you can find a consistent pace and float through the forest. If wanting more mileage, run the loop twice before

crossing back over the bridge, or choose one of the additional trails within the park to extend your route. Once finished, consider taking your shoes and socks off and wading in the river shallows, or dangle your legs and feet into the cool river from a rock. Some say the cold water will help to speed muscle recovery. Whether true or not, it certainly feels good on a hot day!

Getting There

The Cox Mountain Trailhead is located within the Fews Ford Access area at the end of Cole Mill Road (northwest of where it crosses Pleasant Green Road). The trailhead begins just off the paved parking lot near the picnic area, where you will find parking and restroom facilities. Additional parking and restrooms are available at the park office that you pass as you first enter the park, which might be helpful if the picnic parking lot is full. There is a short walk down to the trailhead if you choose to park near the office.

Extend Your Trip

Without having to drive to a different parking lot, you can access up to 13 miles of trails at the Fews Ford Access area to extend your day. Canoeing and fishing are also options at the park. Approximately 2.75 miles south of Fews Ford Access, you will find parking and canoe access on Pleasant Green Road, just north of I-85 and US Hwy. 70. From this access point, you can also connect to the moderately challenging Laurel Bluffs Trail, which is part of the NC Mountains-to-Sea Trail. It winds its way along the Eno River for an out-and-back distance of 15.7 total miles and is popular for running, hiking, and birding. If you visit in warmer months, consider wearing or bringing your swimsuit. Along the river, there are kid-friendly swimming holes with shallow flowing water, which are very refreshing on a hot day!

If you want to make it an overnight trip, look into the primitive campsites available. Visit ncparks.gov/state-parks/eno-river-state-park for details and other park information.

Trail Tip: *Plan ahead and calculate the amount of time you need to complete the trail. No matter your skill or fitness level, you should always avoid being on trails you don't know in the dark.*

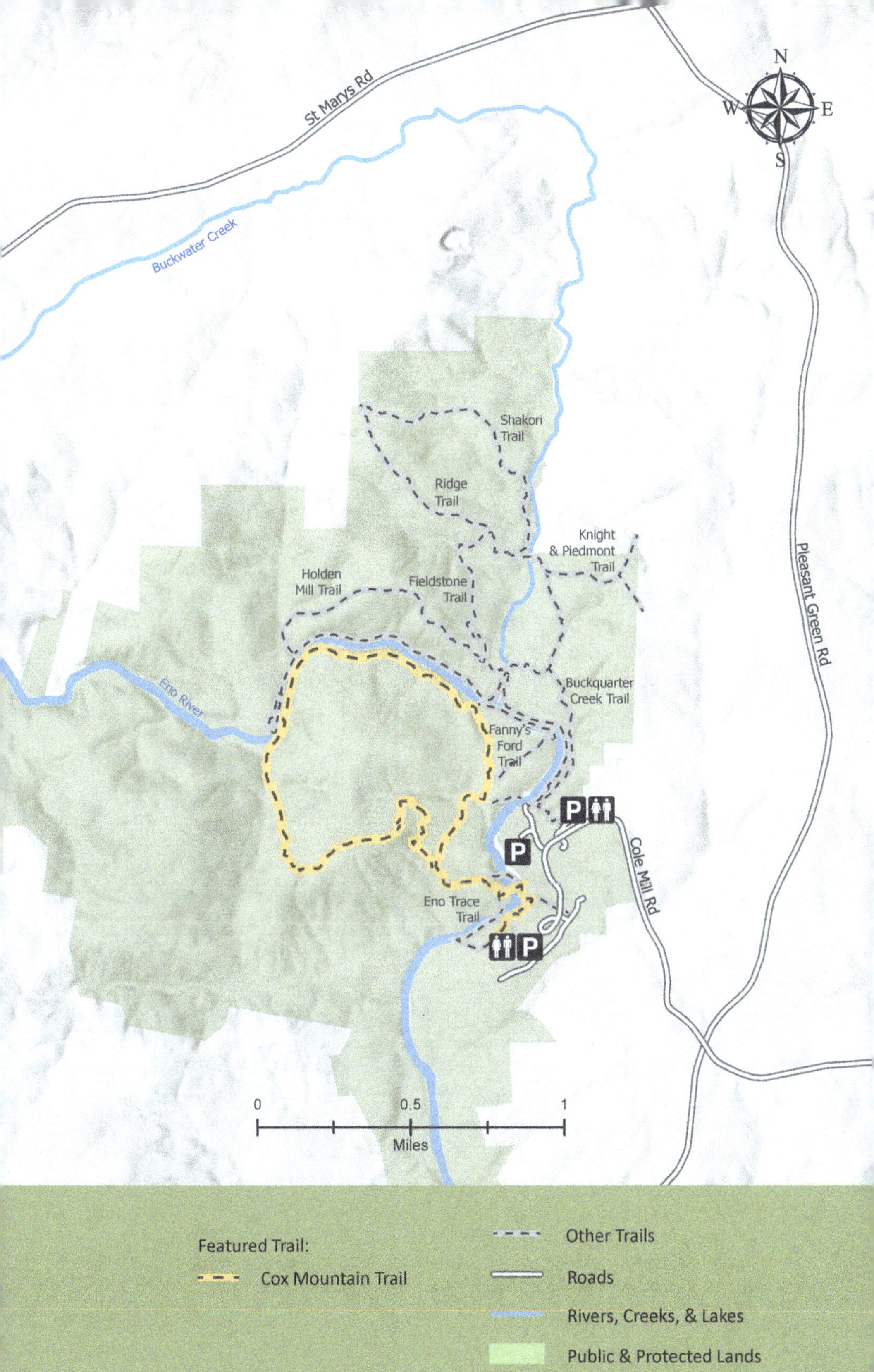

N
W E
S
St Marys Rd
Buckwater Creek
Pleasant Green Rd
Shakori Trail
Ridge Trail
Knight & Piedmont Trail
Holden Mill Trail
Fieldstone Trail
Buckquarter Creek Trail
Eno River
Fanny's Ford Trail
Cole Mill Rd
Eno Trace Trail
0
0.5
1
Miles
Featured Trail:
Cox Mountain Trail
Other Trails
Roads
Rivers, Creeks, & Lakes
Public & Protected Lands

Hungry? Let's Eat!

Guglhupf Bakery, Cafe & Biergarten
2706 Durham-Chapel Hill Blvd., Durham, NC 27707

This German bakery and café is sure to please! Claudia Kemmet-Cooper has made her mark in Durham as co-founder and owner of Guglhupf, sharing her southern German delicacies since 1998 with the opening of the Bakery & Patisserie. Their bakers prepare breads and pastries using the finest ingredients and follow traditional European baking methods. The adjacent café, added in 2004, serves delicious southwestern (Swabian) German fare, sourcing local and seasonal ingredients. Vegetarian, vegan, and wheat-free options are available on the menu. The café space has a unique architectural style, with lower and upper levels of cozy indoor seating, as well as plentiful patio garden tables surrounded by creative plantings and a delightful water feature gracing the entrance. It is a relaxing space, perfect for refueling after time on the trail. The café serves breakfast, brunch, lunch, and dinner. A recent addition is the evening biergarten, with a variety of beers on tap, handcrafted cocktails, and other spirits. Check online for specific hours. Don't forget to take home a little bakery item or two on your way out. The "bretzel" knots are a favorite. Or visit their Chapel Hill Bake Shop, established in 2017, serving coffees, teas, and delicious breads and pastries fresh from the Guglhupf Bakery. Both locations are closed on Monday.

Foster's Market
2694 Durham-Chapel Hill Blvd.,
Durham, NC 27707

Sara Foster has mastered the art of Southern fare. Her irresistible breakfast, lunch, and bakery treats are always crowd pleasers. Warm and inviting, this family-owned, casual neighborhood restaurant has been a staple for the Durham community for over 30 years. With a large outside dining area, or rustic

tables inside, Foster's offers a comfortable space to enjoy your treat or meal made with fresh-from-the-farm ingredients. Their menu touts extensive breakfast items as meals or a-la-carte items, hot and cold sandwiches, wraps, soups, salads, smoothies, and even grilled cheese and PB&J for the kids. Be sure to check out Sara's cookbooks and products for sale in the shop, too!

Do both restaurants sound so good that you can't decide which to try? These two are so close to each other you can walk between them and have lunch at one and get sweet treats from the other!

GOOD MORNING MUFFINS

These delicious and versatile muffins pack in the flavor and the nutrients, with extra protein from the almond flour and an extra boost of fiber and vitamins from the veggies and fruits. Eat them warm or pack them for the trail! Mix and match add-ins, switching out zucchini for the apples (will be less sweet), chocolate chips in place of dried fruit, or add pumpkin seeds or nuts for an extra crunchy texture. These muffins are a sure thing for a good morning!

DRY INGREDIENTS:

1 cup whole wheat pastry flour
    or all-purpose flour
1 cup almond flour
1 ½ cups rolled oats
2 teaspoons cinnamon
1 teaspoon baking soda
½ teaspoon salt
½ cup dried cherries or
    other dried fruit

WET INGREDIENTS:

3 eggs
½ cup maple syrup
6 tablespoons butter, melted
1 cup grated apples
1 cup grated carrots

DIRECTIONS:

Preheat oven to 350°F and line a standard 12-cup muffin pan with paper muffin cups or spray. In a large bowl, mix the dry ingredients together. In a separate bowl, whisk the eggs, then add maple syrup and melted butter, and stir in grated apples and carrots. Add the dry ingredients to the wet ingredients and stir until combined. Scoop the batter into the muffin tin, filling each cup to the brim. Bake for 25 minutes or until the muffins are lightly browned on top and a toothpick comes out clean. Store in an airtight container in the refrigerator for up to a week, or freeze for later.

Little River Regional Park and Natural Area

Distance: **7 miles, multiple loops**
Difficulty Level: **moderate**
Trailhead: **301 Little River Park Way, Rougemont, NC 27572**

There is something infinitely healing in the repeated refrains of nature—
the assurance that dawn comes after night, and spring after winter.
— Rachel Carson

Little River Regional Park and Natural Area is a gem of a place, with a total of 7 miles of trails and options to extend a hike or run on additional mountain bike trails. Our favorite route is to follow the Ridge Trail to the North River Loop Trail and then take the South River Loop to get in a great hike or run. There are multiple scenic views of Little River and up-and-down topography, beautiful in every season. Benches in picturesque spots are comfortable places to take a break and watch the water.

The large parking area includes restrooms and two picnic shelters with grills, as well as lots of open space to relax, a playground for kids, a butterfly garden, a horseshoe pit, and even a group camping site.

More to Know

Covering nearly 400 acres and straddling the Orange and Durham County lines, Little River Regional Park and Natural Area was protected in a partnership with Triangle Land Conservancy, Eno River Association, and Orange and Durham Counties in order to protect water quality. The Little River supports rare aquatic animals, including freshwater mussels that can only live in pristine environments, and is a source of Durham's drinking water supply. The property today is transitioning from a former loblolly forest into a typical Piedmont upland oak-hickory forest.

Running Thoughts

It's a joy to traverse these winding forest trails at any pace. They are shaded with plenty of miles to run, showcasing vistas and the sound of the running river as the trails wind along its edge. In any season, the mostly single-track network will give you a great workout, as the terrain rolls up and down, but never feels too steep. These trails are easy-to-moderate with some rocks and roots to navigate, but the landscape will allow you to fall into a consistent running pace all the way through. Trailheads, a nonprofit organization in Carrboro/Chapel Hill, founded the Little River Trail Runs (7K and 10 mile), held on these trails in January. Proceeds benefit the park and trail system.

Getting There

As you arrive at the park off Guess Road, the entrance is easy to spot with the park's logo and stonework signage welcoming you down the short drive to the large gravel parking lot.

Extend Your Trip

If you are headed down to Durham after your hike or run, Sarah P. Duke Gardens is a lovely spot any time of year, but especially in the

spring and summer. Nearly 5 miles of winding paths beautifully showcase an endless variety of colorful flowers, shrubs, and trees. The garden is free, but you will need to pay for parking. Pair a visit here with a stop at Duke University's Nasher Museum of Art.

Hungry? Let's Eat!

Head to Durham's Ninth Street District, located only 20 minutes away from Little River Regional Park and Natural Area, for a wide variety of delicious ways to refuel. With more than 30 establishments to choose from, there's something to please everyone. Round out your day browsing in the many eclectic shops around the district, all walkable with a friendly neighborhood feel. On-street parking is generally easy to find on Ninth Street and surrounding streets. Find more information at discover9thstreet.com.

Some of our favorite places to eat include:

Mad Hatter's Café and Bakeshop
1802 W. Main St., Durham, NC 27705
Whether you are feeling savory or sweet, Mad Hatter's is going to please. Brunch is served all day, and there are many mouthwatering choices of sandwiches, salads, and bakery treats, all prepared on-site. Stop in for your morning coffee and breakfast item, or make it your lunchtime choice, dining indoors or on an outside patio. While there, you may catch a glimpse of the pastry chefs hard at work decorating elaborate cakes behind the bakery counter. It's quite a treat itself to watch them create!

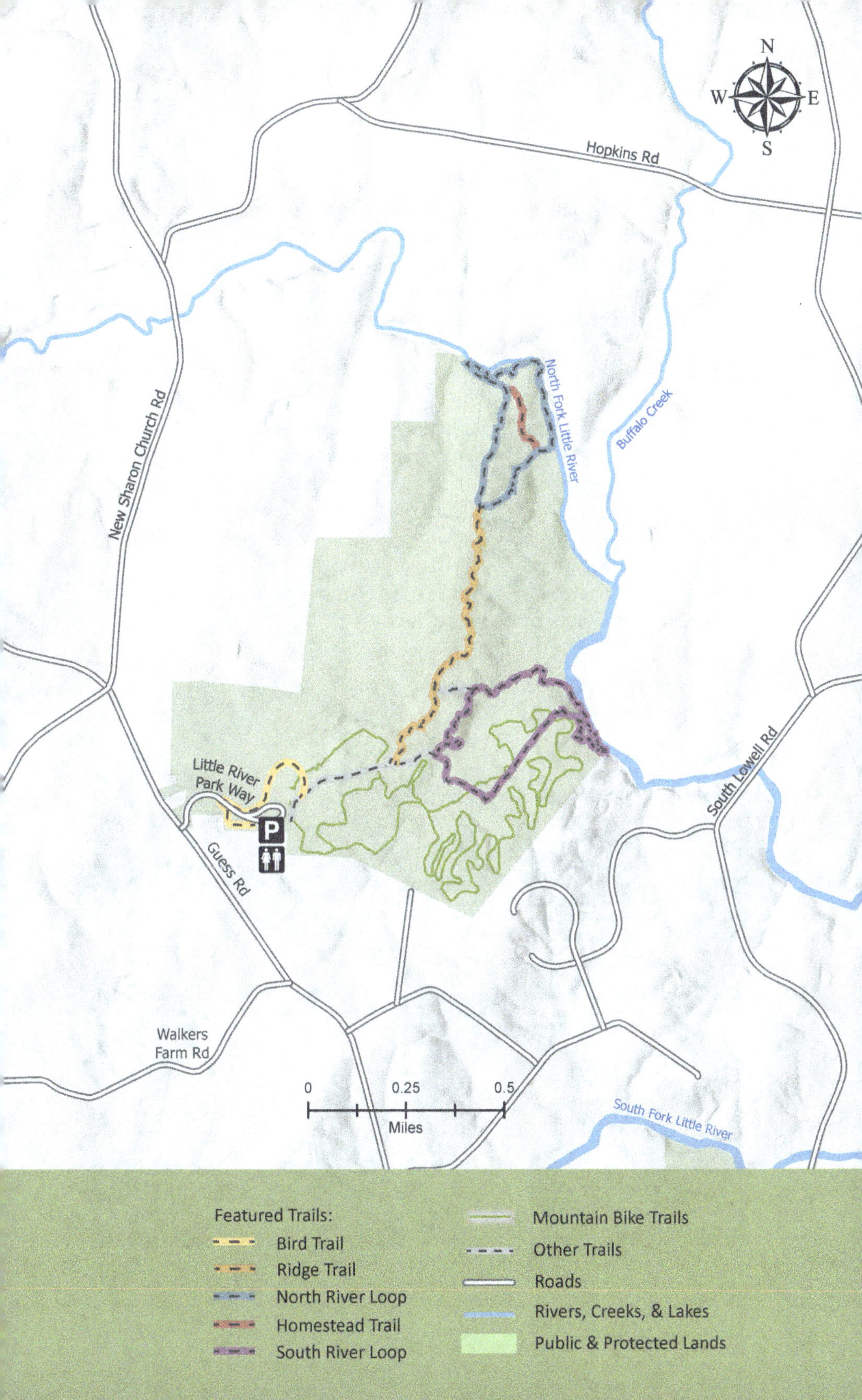

N
W E
S
Hopkins Rd
New Sharon Church Rd
North Fork Little River
Buffalo Creek
South Lowell Rd
Little River Park Way
P
Guess Rd
Walkers Farm Rd
South Fork Little River
0
0.25
0.5
Miles
Featured Trails:
Bird Trail
Ridge Trail
North River Loop
Homestead Trail
South River Loop
Mountain Bike Trails
Other Trails
Roads
Rivers, Creeks, & Lakes
Public & Protected Lands

Elmo's Diner
776 Ninth St., Durham, NC 27705

This kid-friendly diner serves breakfast (all day) and lunch in a lively atmosphere, with seating in comfy booths and tables. To keep your little ones happy while you wait for your order, Elmo's offers crayons and coloring sheets of their namesake duck. The diner's made-from-scratch mentality and friendly service makes this place a great choice any day of the week. Hollis recommends the blueberry pancakes!

Cosmic Cantina
1920 Perry St., Durham, NC 27705

This hard-to-find cantina is located on Perry Street just off Ninth Street. It's a lofty climb up a flight of stairs amid graffiti to get to the restaurant, but this late-night college hangout is classic and worth the climb. Cosmic's burritos will put a smile on your face and curb that post-hike hunger. They offer many meat, vegan, and veggie options, touting organic ingredients, and are known for their tasty margaritas served in a plastic cup. Cosmic offers a funky, laid-back atmosphere with indoor seating available, or, on a nice day, head outside and enjoy your meal on the deck.

Company Mill Trail, William B. Umstead State Park

Distance: **5.8 miles, lollipop loop**
Difficulty Level: **moderate**
Trailhead: **Reedy Creek Entrance, 2100 N. Harrison Ave., Cary, NC 27513**

I go to nature to be soothed and healed, and to have my senses put in order.
— John Burroughs

Umstead State Park is a truly peaceful oasis in the middle of one of North Carolina's most highly urbanized areas. Bordered by two busy highways, I-40 and US Hwy. 70, and the Raleigh-Durham International Airport, the park spreads across 5,600 acres, creating an unparalleled wilderness escape.

The Company Mill Trail is one of the park's longest trails and a favorite of many locals. It is named after a mill, originally constructed in 1810 and in operation until the 1900s, that was used for grinding wheat and corn. You will see the remains of the mill's dam by Crabtree Creek. The trail is mostly shaded, and it is well marked with square, orange blazes. Company Mill has moderate ups and downs and follows parts of Sycamore and Crabtree Creeks. It begins at the Shelter 1 Picnic Area in the northern corner of the parking lot, just past the restrooms. One mile in, the trail crosses Crabtree Creek on a very sturdy footbridge, and there the loop begins. (You can go either way.) If you want to shorten the loop, skip the section along Sycamore Creek by taking the Reedy Creek Multi-use Trail.

Before you start your hike or run, visit the educational signs that provide information about the history and biology in the park. They are located near the well-maintained restrooms and water fountains next to the main parking lot. On the way to the bridge from the parking lot, consider taking the short interpretive trail off to the left called Inspiration Point, which has benches and tree identification markers.

More to Know

Once managed as timberland, this area was first developed for recreation use by the Civilian Conservation Corps (CCC) in the 1930s, the Depression-era program that provided much-needed jobs. In fact, the CCC developed four of North Carolina's most iconic state parks: Fort Macon, Hanging Rock, Mount Mitchell, and Morrow Mountain; and two national parks, Great Smoky Mountains and Cape Hatteras. At all these parks, you can see the CCC's quality work to this day.

The area of Umstead State Park was managed as two segregated parks from 1950 to 1964, Crabtree Creek State Park for whites and Reedy Creek State Park for Blacks. A noticeable remnant of the segregation of entrances is the lack of a connecting road.

Trail Tip: *Become familiar with your trail before you start the hike. Spend some time online and look at maps or brochures so you can consider length, difficulty level, elevation, and terrain. Determine where you will park and where the restrooms are located. Decide whether you want to take a loop trail, so you wind up back where you started, or an out-and-back path that will require you to retrace your steps.*

The East Coast Greenway, a 3,000-mile-long system of trails connecting Maine to Florida, runs through the park along the Reedy Creek Multi-use Trail. In North Carolina, the East Coast Greenway travels 366 miles on its spine route through the Triangle, to Fayetteville, and then Wilmington. Currently there are 102 miles of greenway on the ground, including the section in Umstead State Park. There is also a Historic Coastal Route. It enters North Carolina from Virginia on the Dismal Swamp Canal Trail and follows the coast, connecting Greenville and Jacksonville before reaching Wilmington and joining the spine route.

Running Thoughts

This technical single-track trail will keep you watching your footing carefully. The roots and rocks are part of the allure of Company Mill. There are also gently rolling and smooth sections of the trail, covered with soft pine straw. Remember to look up and take in the beauty of the forest and the creeks as you go. Pace yourself for a long run, and consider adding several faster-paced, 30-to-60-second pickups sprinkled into your run to keep it interesting. It is helpful to bring water with you in a pack, on a belt, or in a handheld bottle since this run can easily take over an hour.

Getting There

To access the Company Mill Trail, enter Umstead State Park through the Reedy Creek Entrance. This entrance is located on Harrison Avenue in Cary, approximately 0.25 miles off I-40 at Exit 287.

Extend Your Trip

Enter the park from the Crabtree Entrance to reach the visitor center and gift shop. For a fun side trip from this location, visit the park's unique and spectacular chainsaw art. Two artists from Smoky Mountain Art transformed a 25-foot fallen oak tree into amazing carvings of animals, tree branches, and leaves. The art display is located on the Graylyn Multi-use Trail and is approximately a 1-mile walk from the Sycamore parking area. Overall, the park has 13 miles of multi-use trails that are more like gravel roads, suitable for mountain biking and horseback riding. If getting on the water to cool off is high on your list after hiking or running, try nearby Lake Crabtree County Park (1400 Aviation Pkwy., Morrisville, NC 27560), where you can borrow canoes, kayaks, stand-up paddle boards, and pedal boats for up to two hours for no charge (check hours; may be available only Friday, Saturday, and Sunday).

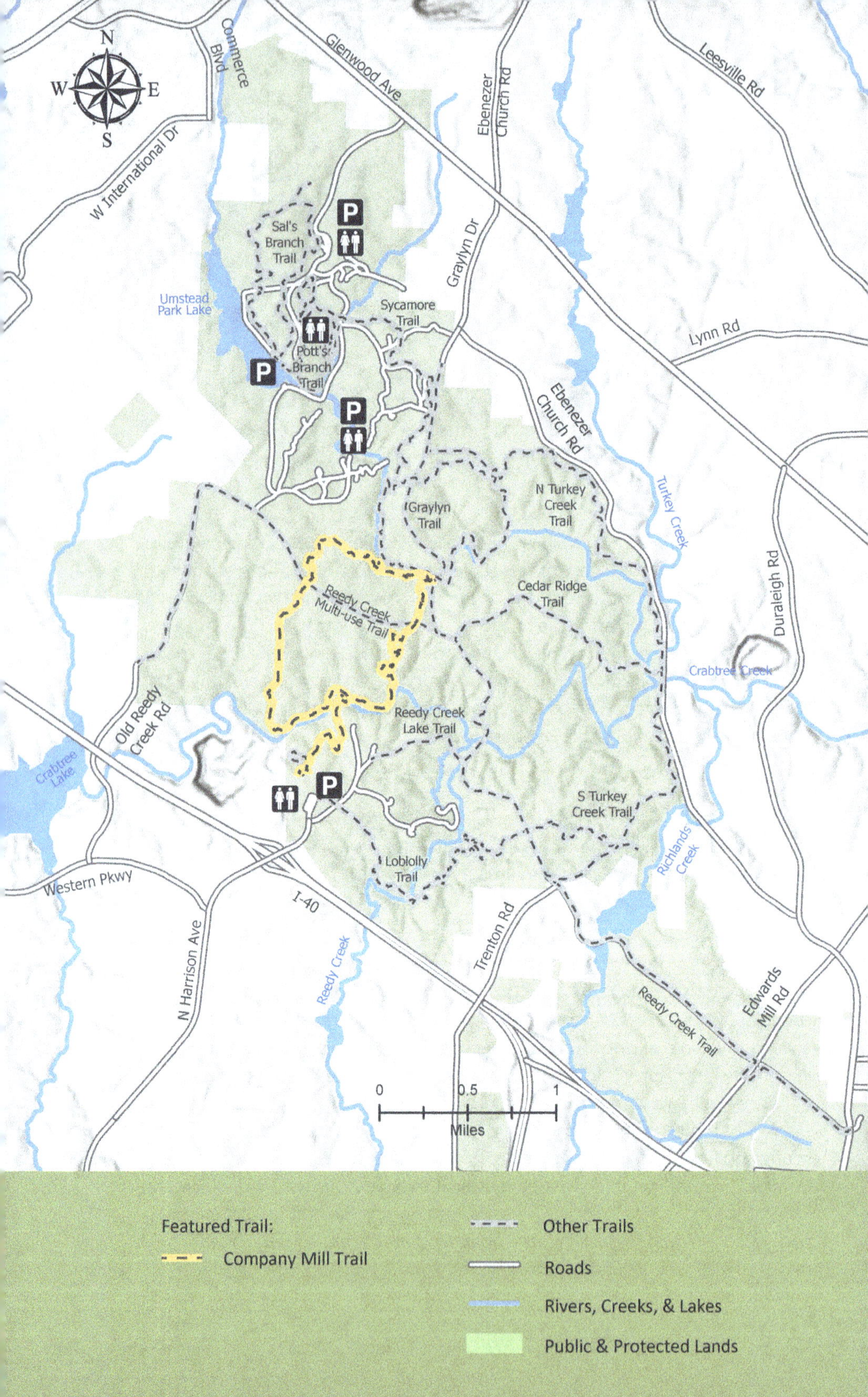

N
W E
S
Commerce Blvd
Glenwood Ave
Ebenezer Church Rd
Leesville Rd
W International Dr
Graylyn Dr
Lynn Rd
Sal's Branch Trail
Umstead Park Lake
Sycamore Trail
Pott's Branch Trail
Ebenezer Church Rd
Graylyn Trail
N Turkey Creek Trail
Turkey Creek
Duraleigh Rd
Reedy Creek Multi-use Trail
Cedar Ridge Trail
Crabtree Creek
Old Reedy Creek Rd
Reedy Creek Lake Trail
Crabtree Lake
S Turkey Creek Trail
Richlands Creek
Western Pkwy
Loblolly Trail
I-40
N Harrison Ave
Trenton Rd
Reedy Creek
Reedy Creek Trail
Edwards Mill Rd
0   0.5   1
Miles
Featured Trail:
Company Mill Trail
Other Trails
Roads
Rivers, Creeks, & Lakes
Public & Protected Lands

Hungry? Let's Eat!

There are many options for sweet and savory treats in Cary, only a few minutes' drive from the Umstead trails. Discover your favorites! Dame's Chicken and Waffles and Pizzeria Faulisi are a couple of additional choices to consider after your trail adventure.

La Farm Bakery – Preston Corners
4248 N.W. Cary Pkwy., Cary, NC 27513

Not far from our featured trail is a French bakery that is worth exploring any day of the week. La Farm Bakery, established in 1999 and named after a gristmill, creates made-from-scratch artisan breads, pastries, baked goods, brunch items, and breakfast and lunch sandwiches. Their signature loaf is a light sourdough handcrafted in 5-pound boules in a three-day process, and is available for purchase in whole, half, or quarter loaves. They use North Carolina-grown, cold-stone milled, organic, heirloom flours, and locally sourced ingredients from the State Farmers Market in Raleigh as well as many other North Carolina businesses. The coffee and espresso served is from Durham's locally roasted Counter Culture Coffee. La Farm's founder and Maître Boulanger (master baker), Lionel Vatinet, trained in France with the centuries-old artisans guild Les Compagnons du Devoir. With his hard-earned title, knowledge, and passion for breads and baking, he has devoted his life to teaching, sharing, and preserving the art and science of the trade. Try La Farm's incredible bakery selections from one of three locations in Cary, or find their breads in many Whole Foods stores in the Triangle. Check out the master baker's book, *A Passion for Bread*, or even attend a baking class.

Raleigh Brewing at the Arboretum
2036 Renaissance Park Pl., Cary, NC 27513

This female-owned business has over 10 years of brewing history. Kristie Nystedt was the first woman in North Carolina to own a craft brewery. Raleigh Brewing, open 7 days a week, offers customers a full selection of beer choices: signature beers (available all year), seasonal beers, small batch beers (available to taproom customers only), and even their own root beer. Want a bite to eat with your beverage? Located in the taproom, Chelsea Café and Catering is ready to serve you Tuesday through Saturday. Curb your post-trail hunger with deli sandwiches, paninis, wraps, quesadillas, Bavarian pretzels, and other pub fare items. Bring your canine; this brewing company is dog-friendly. Raleigh Brewing at the Arboretum has weekly events, including trivia night, cycle club, and yes, run club. Visit their website for details at raleighbrewing.com. Check out their taproom location on Neil Street in Raleigh, too, home of the production facility. We love that Raleigh Brewing supports local events, including the Sir Walter Miler, a track-based event held every August in Raleigh.

Ann and Jim Goodnight Museum Park, NC Museum of Art

Distance: **up to 4.7 miles, multiple loops**
Difficulty Level: **easy**
Trailhead: **2110 Blue Ridge Rd., Raleigh, NC 27607**

Land really is the best art.
— Andy Warhol

The Ann and Jim Goodnight Museum Park, known as the "Museum Park," is located on the 164-acre North Carolina Museum of Art campus. This urban park and connection to Reedy Creek Trail can be an all-day adventure, filled with exercise, art, culture, and relaxation. Bring along your walking or running shoes, dog, bike, picnic, and creative mind. There are many ways to customize your day here. Visit the sculptures, pond platform (a project with NC State University's School of Architecture), outdoor theater, welcome center, and sustainable landscape and irrigation system. Escape along the winding dirt and paved paths and discover 30 different art installations. In the wooded section of the campus along House Creek, follow the Reedy Creek Trail to the impressive 660-foot-long, 12-foot-wide pedestrian and bicycle bridge over I-440 with additional trail connections.

More to Know

The park is open 365 days per year, dawn to dusk. There are unique events throughout the year, including music performances in the outdoor theater, movies on the large outdoor screen, a not-to-miss annual lantern walk in December, full moon walks, regular tours on weekends, Tai Chi, yoga classes, and more. The Museum galleries may lure you inside and entry is free except for special exhibits. Check schedules and prices online when planning your visit.

Running Thoughts

New to running? This is a great place to start. These are smooth dirt and some paved trail surfaces. Run between sculptures and catch your breath while you study and read the marker about each work. Include a stop at the theater for a sip of water at the fountain, and stretch in the shaded grove when you are finished. Or, if you are a seasoned triathlete or new to the sport, bring your bike and get in a "brick" session, biking the Reedy Creek Greenway and then running the Museum Park paths.

Getting There

The NC Museum of Art is located just off Wade Avenue and Raleigh's I-440 beltline. Ample parking is available at the museum entrance on Blue Ridge Road in two large, paved lots that are free to the public and an easy walk to the trails. Wheelchair-accessible parking is available. Restrooms and water fountains are on-site at the Joseph M. Bryan, Jr. Theater as well as at the welcome center. A detailed map listing the works of art you will find along the trail can be picked up once you arrive, or you can view it online.

Extend Your Trip

The 4.7-mile Reedy Creek Greenway crosses through the Museum Park, with connections to the west and east. To the west, the trail follows Reedy Creek Road as a protected side path, passing Prairie Ridge Ecostation, NC State University's Equine Farm, and Schenck Forest, ending at Umstead State Park. To the east, after crossing the pedestrian bridge over I-440, the Reedy Creek Greenway connects to Meredith College and NC State University. The Reedy Creek Greenway is a designated section of the East Coast Greenway route. In the Triangle area, more than 68 continuous miles of the East Coast Greenway are off-road, extending from Durham to Clayton. This stretch includes the American Tobacco Trail, Umstead State Park, the Museum Park, and the Neuse River Greenway.

Trail Tip: *It's great to run/hike fast, but sometimes, slow is better. Take it all in.*

Hungry? Let's Eat!

East Café
2110 Blue Ridge Rd., Raleigh, NC 27607
The East Café at the NC Museum of Art is in the East Building on the ground level, and it overlooks the park expanse. You do not have to enter the museum to access the café. It offers a relaxing outdoor patio space with colorful umbrella tables. Or you could enjoy the indoor space, with fresh flowers on each table and a nice view through the large glass windows. Drinks (beer, wine, soft drinks, tea, coffees) and light lunch options are available for purchase.

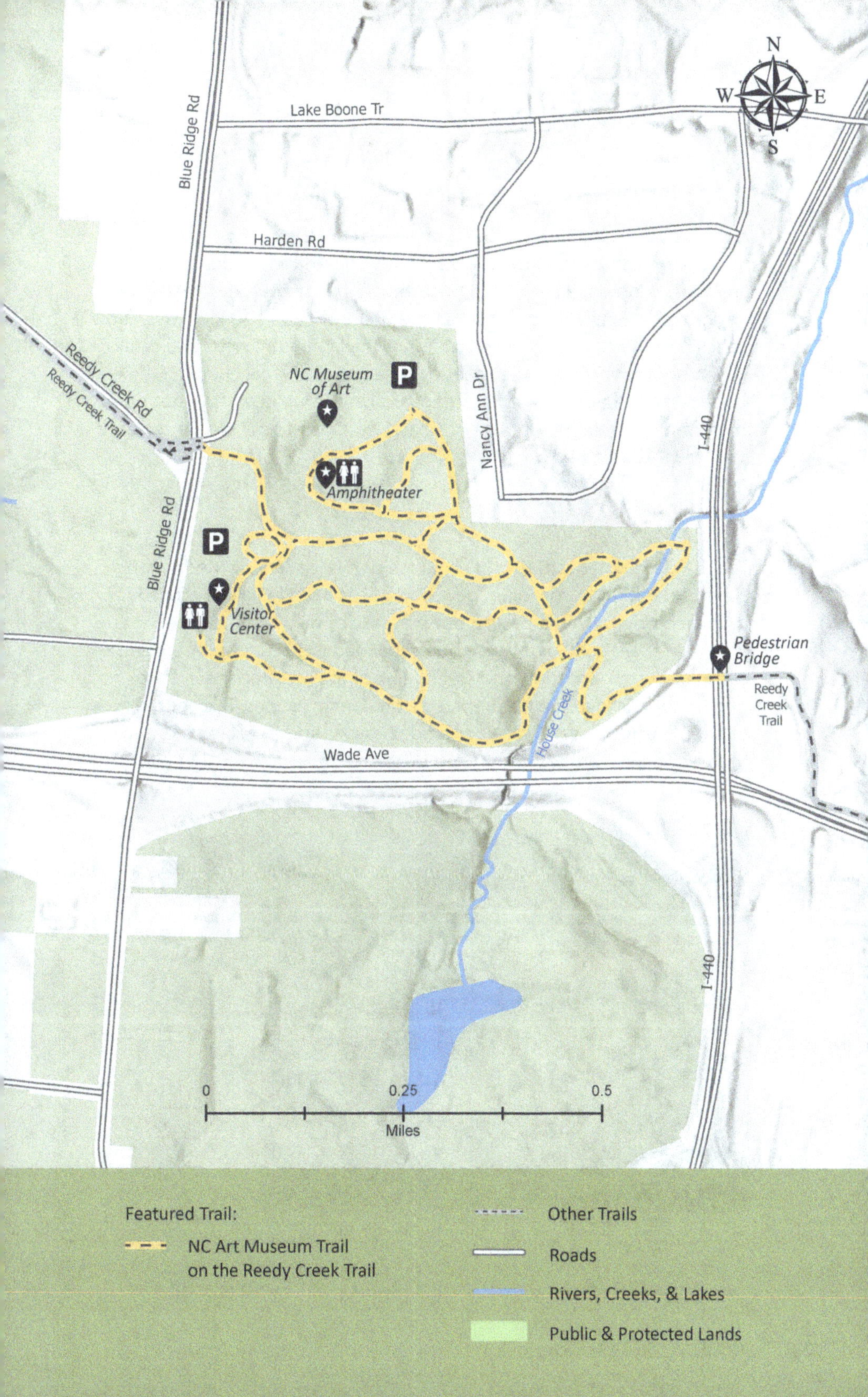

N
W E
S
Blue Ridge Rd
Lake Boone Tr
Harden Rd
Nancy Ann Dr
I-440
Reedy Creek Rd
Reedy Creek Trail
P
NC Museum of Art
Amphitheater
P
Visitor Center
Blue Ridge Rd
Pedestrian Bridge
Reedy Creek Trail
House Creek
Wade Ave
I-440
0
0.25
0.5
Miles
Featured Trail:
NC Art Museum Trail on the Reedy Creek Trail
Other Trails
Roads
Rivers, Creeks, & Lakes
Public & Protected Lands

Looking for other options nearby?

Char-Grill
3211 Edwards Mill Rd., Raleigh, NC 27612 (in Olde Raleigh Village)
A throwback to the 1960s, Char-Grill has several Raleigh locations, and one only a few minutes from the Museum Park. This Triangle mainstay serves up a darn good burger and fries to curb your hunger quickly. The fun here begins by marking your order on a little sheet of paper, using a tiny yellow pencil (like the ones they used to have at the library near the card catalogs, remember those?). Slide the sheet down a stainless-steel chute to the chefs inside. Watch them make your order through the window. Take out or eat at the red picnic tables outside of Char-Grill. Don't forget a thick, creamy milkshake. You earned it today!

Neomonde Mediterranean Cafe
3817 Beryl Rd., Raleigh, NC 27607
This is a delicious, healthy stop for lunch or dinner, serving Mediterranean cuisine. Neomonde, meaning "new world," has been in Raleigh since 1977. It opened originally as a bakery, tempting customers with fresh Lebanese breads. In the late 1980s, Neomonde expanded the business, opening the deli in its current location on Beryl Road, serving Mediterranean foods made from authentic ingredients, prepared from family recipes. Take-out, dine-in, or patio seating is available. Neomonde has two additional locations in Morrisville and Durham.

Relax on the East Café patio with a beverage or lunch and a beautiful view of the museum grounds.

23 Bailey and Sarah Williamson Preserve

Distance: **up to 16 miles, multiple loops**
Difficulty Level: **easy**
Trailhead: **4409 Mial Plantation Rd., Raleigh, NC 27610**

Leave the road, take the trails.
            — Pythagoras

Escape the hustle and bustle of life into peaceful tranquility at Triangle Land Conservancy's Bailey and Sarah Williamson Preserve on the east side of Raleigh near Clayton. With 447 acres of land, the preserve has one of the most extensive multi-use trail networks in the Triangle region. It includes 16 miles of trails on multiple loops, providing flexibility for those who are looking for a short excursion or those seeking much longer adventures.

The extensive network means there's a lot of room for people to spread out. The well-marked trails roll and meander through meadows and pine and hardwood forests, with some interesting rock formations, stream crossings, and added features for mountain bikers. Don't miss the peaceful Two Pond Loop (no bikes) to look for great blue herons and sunning turtles. There's even a spot by the pond to hang a hammock. On our map, we feature Walnut Hill Way, Pine Warbler Trail, Little Falls Loop, and a return on the Two Pond Loop, for a total of almost 4.5 miles. There are additional loops and a connector to the Clayton River Walk to extend your adventure.

Because the trails are open to mountain biking, trail running, and hiking, there is a simple system to reduce user conflicts: Sunday through Wednesday, walkers turn right at trail intersections, and bikers and runners turn left. Thursday through Saturday, walkers turn left, and bikers and runners turn right. Don't worry about remembering this; the information is well posted in multiple places at the preserve to keep you headed the right way!

The trails are closed when wet. Be sure to check the Triangle Land Conservancy website (triangleland.org) before heading there.

More to Know

The Williamson Preserve fulfills Bailey and Sarah Williamson's dream to protect land that had been in their family for more than two centuries and once was one of the largest cotton plantations in the area. In addition to trails, the tract of land serves as a hub for sustainable agriculture. The Williamson Preserve hosts several new and beginning farmers who participate in regenerative cattle grazing, native plant propagation, and small-scale produce production. Another goal is to use farm resources for community food support. The new agriculture pavilion provides space for farmers to process, pack, and store their products on-site. It is also available for educational and other events.

Signage at the preserve and in the white barn shares the history of the preserve, its land and the Williamson family, as well as information on the Tuscarora tribe, plantation and tobacco farming, and Black rural land ownership in the area.

Trail Tip: *Poison ivy: know what it looks like and stay away from it. Keep this in mind: leaves of three, let it be and don't touch the hairy vines. Poison ivy vines are toxic even in the winter.*

Running Thoughts

The space is peaceful, and the forest is so quiet. It's a great day for a zen run. Leave your watch behind today and just run the trails at a pace that feels good. Let your body and mind be immersed in the forest sights, sounds and smells, and take it all in. The Japanese practice of forest bathing (shinrin-yoku) can have many health benefits. Spending time in nature can reduce your tension level, lower your blood pressure, and boost your mood.

Getting There

The Williamson Preserve is located on the east side of Wake County, between the fast-growing communities of Knightdale and Clayton, off I-87, with a large, clearly marked parking lot on Mial Plantation Road. The preserve is gaining popularity, so try to come during off hours, because there is no overflow parking allowed on the road. The gates to the large parking lot are shut when the trails are closed due to wet conditions. There is a portable toilet on-site.

Extend Your Trip

The Williamson Preserve directly connects to the Clayton River Walk along the Neuse River. If you don't want to walk/run/bike the longer distance within the preserve to get to the River Walk, you can directly access the trail at a parking area located 3 miles down Mial Plantation Road toward Clayton. This gorgeous, paved greenway follows the Neuse River for about 4 miles, ending close to Clayton's downtown, with an attractive pedestrian bridge across the river on the way. The River Walk is part of the 27.5-mile Neuse River Greenway, which begins at Falls Lake Dam and ends at Clayton. There are multiple points of entry along the greenway, which offer scenic views of the Neuse River, winding boardwalk areas through wetlands, historical sites, interpretive signs, and agricultural fields. The Neuse River Greenway is a segment of the NC Mountains-to-Sea Trail and the East Coast Greenway.

Hungry? Let's Eat!

Clayton Bakery & Café
8970 US 70 BUS Hwy., Ste. 200, Clayton, NC 27520
Since 2005, this family-owned bakery has been creating delicious baked goods and beverages for their customers. The attentive staff is ready to serve you your morning coffee or pick-me-up treat after a hike. Clayton Bakery & Café uses the finest all-natural, locally sourced ingredients as often as

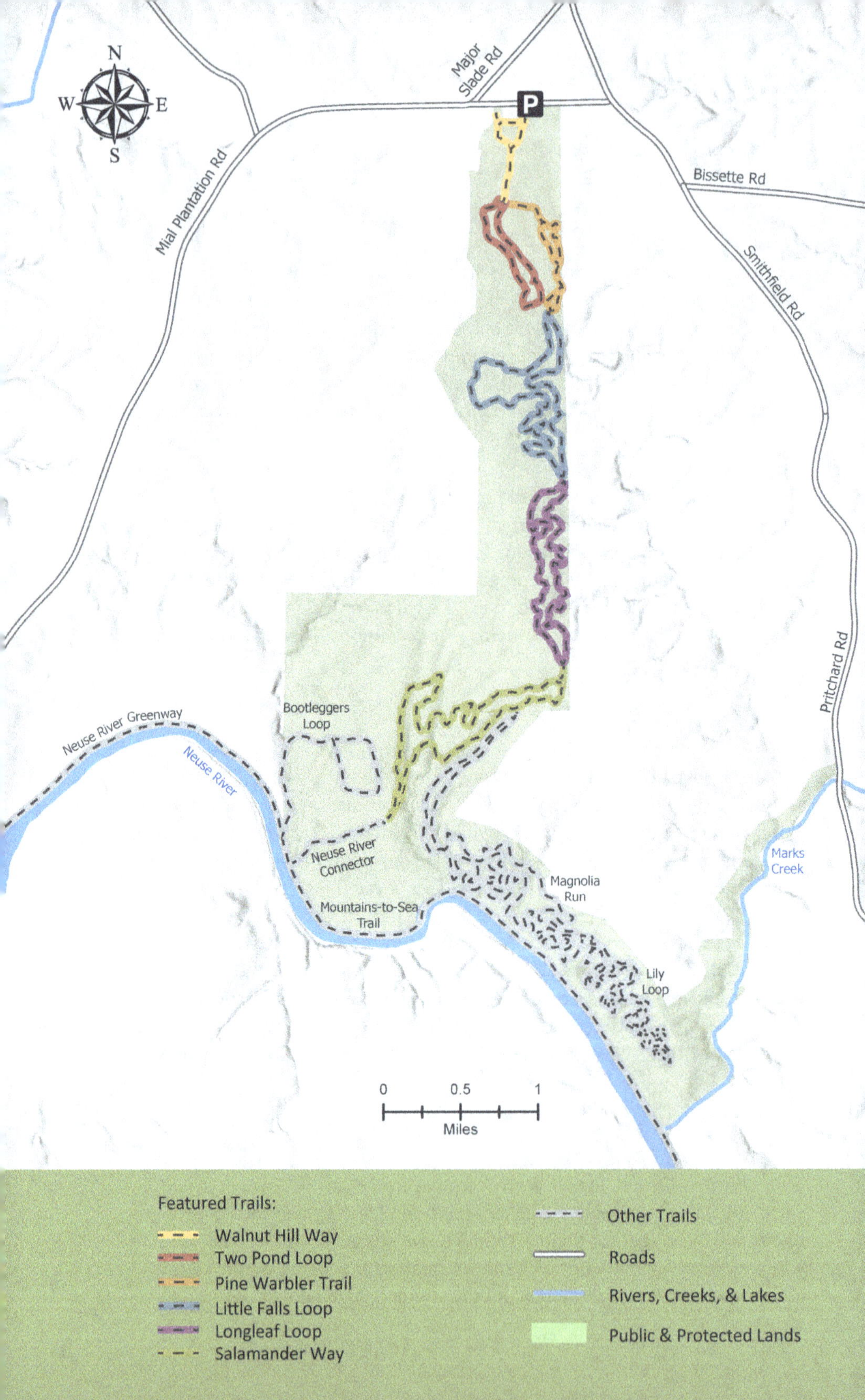

N
W E
S
Major Slade Rd
P
Bissette Rd
Smithfield Rd
Mial Plantation Rd
Pritchard Rd
Bootleggers Loop
Neuse River Greenway
Neuse River
Neuse River Connector
Mountains-to-Sea Trail
Magnolia Run
Marks Creek
Lily Loop
0   0.5   1
Miles
Featured Trails:
Walnut Hill Way
Two Pond Loop
Pine Warbler Trail
Little Falls Loop
Longleaf Loop
Salamander Way
Other Trails
Roads
Rivers, Creeks, & Lakes
Public & Protected Lands

possible, so treat yourself and choose from sweet items, such as muffins, sticky buns, cookies, pies, and cakes, to delicious savory paninis and sandwiches on fresh homemade breads, quiche, soups, and other delights. Take a fresh loaf home. Brought your pup? They make dog treats, too! Closed on Sunday and Monday.

Jones Café
415 E. Main St., Clayton, NC 27520

Jones Café, established in 1958, has been serving up hot dogs and burgers to locals and visitors alike ever since. Back in the day, hot dogs were 15¢ and bottle drinks were 10¢. Things have changed a little since then, but you can be sure that it still has that hometown-diner feel with friendly staff. Jones Café's black-and-white checkered decor with booths, tables, and bar seating will leave you feeling nostalgic. For a quick bite after your trail adventure, this could be just the spot, or come early for breakfast, but don't show up too late—they close at 2 p.m. Closed on Sunday.

C E Barnes Store
13726 Buffalo Rd., Clayton, NC 27527

Family-owned since 1927, this well-known country store, full of nostalgic memorabilia, sells local products from local businesses, including pickles, jams, craft beer, as well as craft items, and gifts for the home. It prides itself on being a food truck haven, with vendors specializing in coffee, breakfast, barbecue, tacos, crepes, and more, all on a rotating basis. Picnic tables out back make a good spot to enjoy your food or beverage. Fresh fruits and veggies are often available, as well as floral bouquets on occasion. Check their Facebook page for the food truck schedule.

Deep River Brewing Company
700 W. Main St., #102, Clayton, NC 27520

Known as "Johnston County's First Legal Brewery," Deep River Brewing Company and owners Paul and Lynn Auclair have been serving their delicious craft brews since 2013, using locally grown raw materials whenever possible. The taproom has a great vibe, with plenty of space to sit at picnic tables inside or out on the patio. Bring your friends along and try a pint or a flight, get a bite to eat from rotating food trucks on-site, and listen to live music on weekends. Show up on Thursday evenings for their run club. Check their calendar at deepriverbrewing.com for a schedule of events. They are closed on Monday and Tuesday.

KRISTEN'S ENERGY BITES

These are super easy to make and are a high-energy snack before you hike
or run. Or pack them for a perfect pick-me-up to eat during or after your
adventure. They will keep up to a week in the refrigerator, but most likely
they'll be devoured well before then.

INGREDIENTS:

1 cup dry rolled oats
2/3 cup unsweetened coconut
    flakes
1/2 cup creamy peanut butter
1/3 cup ground flax seed
1/3 cup chocolate chips
    (mini chips work well)
1/3 cup honey
1 tablespoon wheat germ
1 teaspoon vanilla extract

DIRECTIONS:

Preheat oven to 250°F. Spread
coconut flakes on a cookie sheet
and bake for 8–10 minutes or until
lightly golden brown. Allow toasted
coconut to cool. In a medium bowl,
stir all ingredients together, including
the coconut. Cover and let the
mixture chill in the refrigerator for
an hour. Roll into bite-size balls, and
store in an airtight container in the
refrigerator. (They don't have to be
kept cool in your day pack on the
trail, but they are less sticky at cooler
temperatures.)

Fall Mountain Trail, Morrow Mountain State Park

Distance: **4.1 miles, loop**
Difficulty Level: **moderate**
Trailhead: **49104 Morrow Mountain Rd., Albemarle, NC 28001**

We don't inherit the earth from our ancestors, we borrow it from our children.
— Native American proverb

Of the many trails at Morrow Mountain State Park, our favorite is the Fall Mountain Trail. It shows off the best of the Uwharrie region, starting off with gorgeous views along the edge of the Yadkin River/Lake Tillery, paired with expansive vistas from the summit ridge. This relatively quiet 4.1-mile loop trail begins and ends at the water access parking lot. We recommend following the trail in a counterclockwise direction, with the start located next to the boathouse and restrooms. Orange triangles clearly mark its entire distance. Once departing the lakeside, the trail gains approximately 600 feet in elevation climbing to the top of Fall Mountain. Look for a side path at the top to catch views of the surrounding mountains and lake below. On the way down, you will find a short side path to the historic Kron family cemetery in the woods.

More to Know

Morrow Mountain State Park is in the heart of the ancient Uwharrie Mountains. (See Chapter 11 for more background on the Uwharrie Mountains.) It is located on Lake Tillery, where the Yadkin River joins the Uwharrie River to form the Pee Dee River. Much of the infrastructure in Morrow Mountain State Park was originally constructed by the Civilian Conservation Corps in the 1930s, including the only North Carolina state park day-use swimming pool.

Morrow Mountain is made of rhyolite, a stone easily shaped. Rhyolite was used by indigenous peoples from all over to make arrowheads, spear points, and stone tools. In fact, the famed Hardaway archaeological site, located nearby, is referred to as the "Remington Arms Factory of 10,000 BC," contributing to Morrow Mountain's reputation as one of the most extensive prehistoric quarries in the United States. The mountain also has plentiful supplies of argillite, which was used by the Civilian Conservation Corps to create many of the park's structures.

Trail Tip: Did you know trail etiquette is a thing? Hikers going uphill have the right of way. Hikers yield to runners, bikers, and horses.

Running Thoughts

The park is a an ideal place for peaceful, reflective trail miles. The Fall Mountain Trail loop can be combined with other trails in the park to get basically any mileage you need for a long run. Pick up a copy of the park map or take a photo of the map on your phone and use it to create a route to fit the distance you want to run. These trails are loaded with interesting discoveries along the way. Take your run at a leisurely pace so you won't miss the amazing forest ecosystem and stellar views of the water. Be on the lookout for birds, turtles, snails, spiders, lizards, wildflowers, mushrooms, rhyolite, and argillite. Incorporate detours to the Kron cemetery and the well-maintained homestead, using the stops as snack or water breaks.

Getting There

Morrow Mountain State Park is located between Charlotte and the Triad, providing easy access from either area. Entering off Valley Drive, follow Morrow Mountain Road into the park. To reach the Fall Mountain Trail, turn left at the intersection, and follow the park road to the marina.

Extend Your Trip

You can plan a fabulous full day in Morrow Mountain State Park. In addition to a multitude of trails, be sure to drive or hike to the top of Morrow Mountain, where you will find the best views of the surrounding mountains and Piedmont. There are picnic tables, a historic picnic shelter, and a restroom at the summit, providing a scenic spot for your snack or lunch.

You can also rent a canoe or kayak, take a dip in the pool (in season), and visit the Kron Homestead. This historic site was a self-sufficient farm settled by Dr. Francis Kron and family in the 1830s. Dr. Kron, a horticulturalist renowned for his flowers and vegetables, was Stanly County's first physician, traveling by horse and wagon to treat patients. The Kron Homestead, which includes the Kron home, well, office/infirmary, grape arbor, and greenhouse, is well-maintained and offers a glimpse of 19th century frontier life in rural Piedmont, North Carolina.

You may want to plan more than a day trip. In addition to traditional camping, Morrow Mountain offers two-bedroom family cabins that sleep up to six with a kitchen, fireplace, screened porch, picnic table, and grill. Be sure to check out the Badin Road Drive-In theater for old-fashioned family fun, or visit one of the many charming local towns, including Albemarle and Badin.

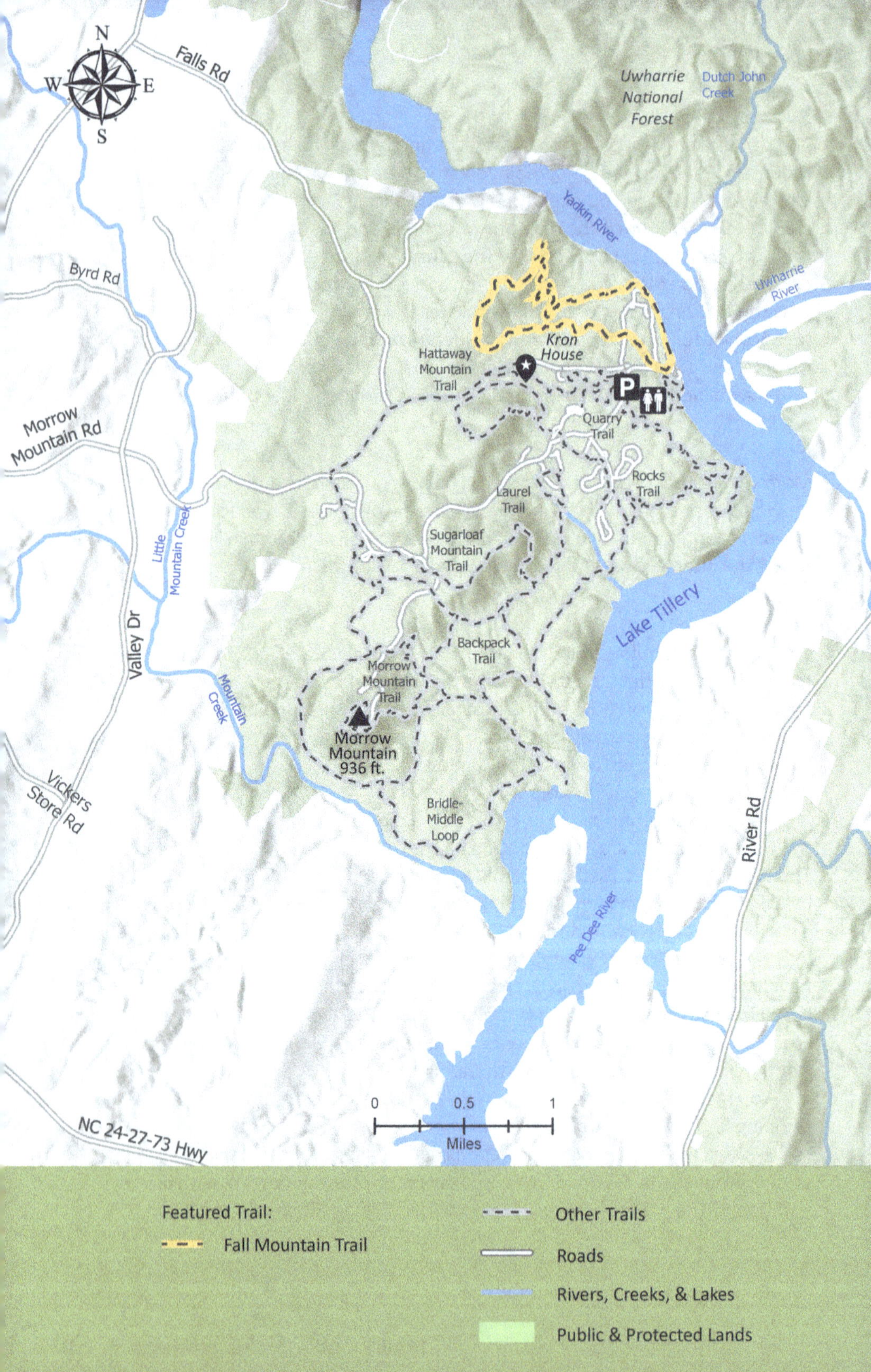

N W E S
Falls Rd
Uwharrie National Forest
Dutch John Creek
Byrd Rd
Yadkin River
Uwharrie River
Morrow Mountain Rd
Kron House
Hattaway Mountain Trail
P
Quarry Trail
Rocks Trail
Little Mountain Creek
Laurel Trail
Valley Dr
Sugarloaf Mountain Trail
Lake Tillery
Mountain Creek
Backpack Trail
Morrow Mountain Trail
Morrow Mountain 936 ft.
Bridle-Middle Loop
Vickers Store Rd
River Rd
Pee Dee River
NC 24-27-73 Hwy
0   0.5   1
Miles
Featured Trail:
Fall Mountain Trail
Other Trails
Roads
Rivers, Creeks, & Lakes
Public & Protected Lands

Hungry? Let's Eat!

Moonset General Store
32254 Valley Dr., Albemarle, NC 28001

This small general store is located near the entrance of the park, making it a nice, close treat. Their friendly staff is ready to scoop delicious Blue Bell Ice Cream for you or make an iced coffee. Moonset carries a host of other drinks, snacks, and candy. Also available at the store is bait, as well as small gift items such as natural, homemade products (soap, candles, etc.), and local honey. They do not have an indoor public restroom. Check ahead for hours, as they are not open every day.

Tho Pizza & Hot Subs
60 Walnut St., Badin, NC 28009

This family-owned restaurant is in the heart of the small, quiet, historic downtown of Badin, located catty-corner to the post office. Tho Pizza & Hot Subs serves tasty takeout, or you can enjoy dining in at one of the small tables inside, or al fresco on the bricked front patio. For a small restaurant and kitchen, their menu is vast and diverse. Choose from Asian dishes such as hibachi, lo mein, fried rice, and teriyaki as well as the standard American fare of wings, pizzas, salads, burgers, and subs. Everything is fresh, delicious, and made-to-order. Treat yourself to lunch or dinner after a great day on Morrow Mountain's trails. Tho is open every day, but note limited hours on Mondays.

Five Points Public House
304 E. Main St., Albemarle, NC 28001

If you are ready to sit inside in a cozy booth, at the bar, or outside on the patio where you can gather around a large wooden table or cozy fire pit, consider the upscale pub atmosphere at Five Points Public House. Located in the charming town of Albemarle, it is open 7 days a week, and appropriately named for being situated at the intersection of five streets. Five Points offers a classic American menu with all the favorites. We love their "Create Your Own Salad" and "Build Your Own Burger" selections. Or perhaps you are ready to splurge with an entree such as filet mignon or grilled salmon. The kids' menu offers a nice selection for your little ones. The bar serves draft and bottled beers, including seasonal craft brews, wines, signature cocktails, and even a creative selection of mules.

McAlpine Creek Park and Greenway

Distance: **3.1 miles (Cross Country Course) and 12.4 miles (Greenway), round trip, out and back**
Difficulty Level: **easy**
Trailhead: **8711 Monroe Rd., Charlotte, NC 28212**

Of all the paths you take in life, make sure a few of them are dirt.
— John Muir

Tucked behind trees off Monroe Road in southeast Charlotte, this hidden gem is not your typical regional park. Rather than ballfields and playgrounds, you will find wide open spaces and a delightful natural surface trail network winding through woods and around two ponds. At the water's edge, you may spot tadpoles, turtles sunning on logs, heron, and other waterfowl looking for their next meal. McAlpine Creek Park is a central point along the McAlpine Creek Greenway, which stretches for 6.2 miles from end to end, changing to the Campbell Creek Greenway to the east along the way. If you visit in the spring, you may spot the rare, native, showy, purple dwarf larkspur. Birders, take note: 188 species of birds have been identified along the Greenway. Created in 1978, the McAlpine Creek Greenway was the first public greenway constructed in North Carolina's western Piedmont. We think you will love everything this park has to offer. Bonus: there are two fenced dog parks off the parking lot.

More to Know

Home to the legendary Larry McAfee 5K Cross Country Course, this park hosts races for local high schools and other running organizations throughout the year. It is a coveted space for the greater Charlotte running community as well as for athletes around the state. In 1978 the East Mecklenburg High School cross country coach, Larry McAfee, working in conjunction with Mecklenburg County Parks and Recreation Department, created a plan for a much-needed 5K cross country (XC) course. With the help of his high school runners, he began building it within the wooded park space behind his house. They even built a hill into the landscape partway through the route because every XC course must have a hill challenge! This became the high school state XC course in 1980 and remained so for 22 years.

It is one of the most iconic courses in the Southeast and continues to be home to the very competitive Wendy's Invitational and many other well-known races. Over the years, hundreds of thousands of athletes of all ages and levels have had the thrill of racing here. On October 4, 2019, the course was appropriately dedicated to Coach McAfee. You can find signage with more information as you cross the bridge from the parking lot into the park.

Running Thoughts

McAlpine Park is a great place to get in duathlon training. Run the historic 5K cross country course, which begins by running the length of the open field, then makes a sharp right turn into the woods. A map of the course is available at the trail as well as online. On completion of your run, the extensive greenway provides a safe biking route either direction for an out and back. The park's large parking lot is an easy transition spot right at your car. Or just stick to running the 5K cross country course and complete it as fast or as slow as you want through the official finish arch, which is a permanent fixture. Imagine the final straightaway next to the lake, lined with a crowd cheering you on as you come into the finish chute!

Getting There

The park is located just off Independence Freeway (US Hwy. 74), 15 minutes from Uptown Charlotte. There is a large sign on Monroe Road, with flagpoles marking the park entrance that takes you to a large parking lot with a park ranger station and well-maintained restrooms.

Extend Your Trip

Pack your bikes and combine your hike or run with an easy, round-trip ride up to 12.4 miles on the McAlpine Creek/Campbell Creek Greenway. You can first ride to the end of the McAlpine Greenway, then turn around and ride back through the park and continue on to the Campbell Creek Greenway. Look for the early 20th century ruins of the Lucas Family Grist Mill along the Campbell Creek section of the greenway. For those who want to take the day a little easier, bring a fishing rod and your fishing license. The pond in McAlpine Creek Park is stocked with catfish, largemouth bass, and bluegill, and it has a dock for casting a line or for peaceful relaxing.

Hungry? Let's Eat!

McAlpine Creek Park is just a few miles from historic downtown Matthews, which offers a wide array of shopping and eating options. Anchoring the quaint downtown area is the Matthews Community Farmers Market. Open all year on Saturday mornings with live music, the market is the largest, most diverse, producer-only farmers market in the greater Charlotte area, with all products coming from within 50 miles (except seafood). If you are visiting midweek, stop in to explore Renfrow's Hardware & General Merchandise,

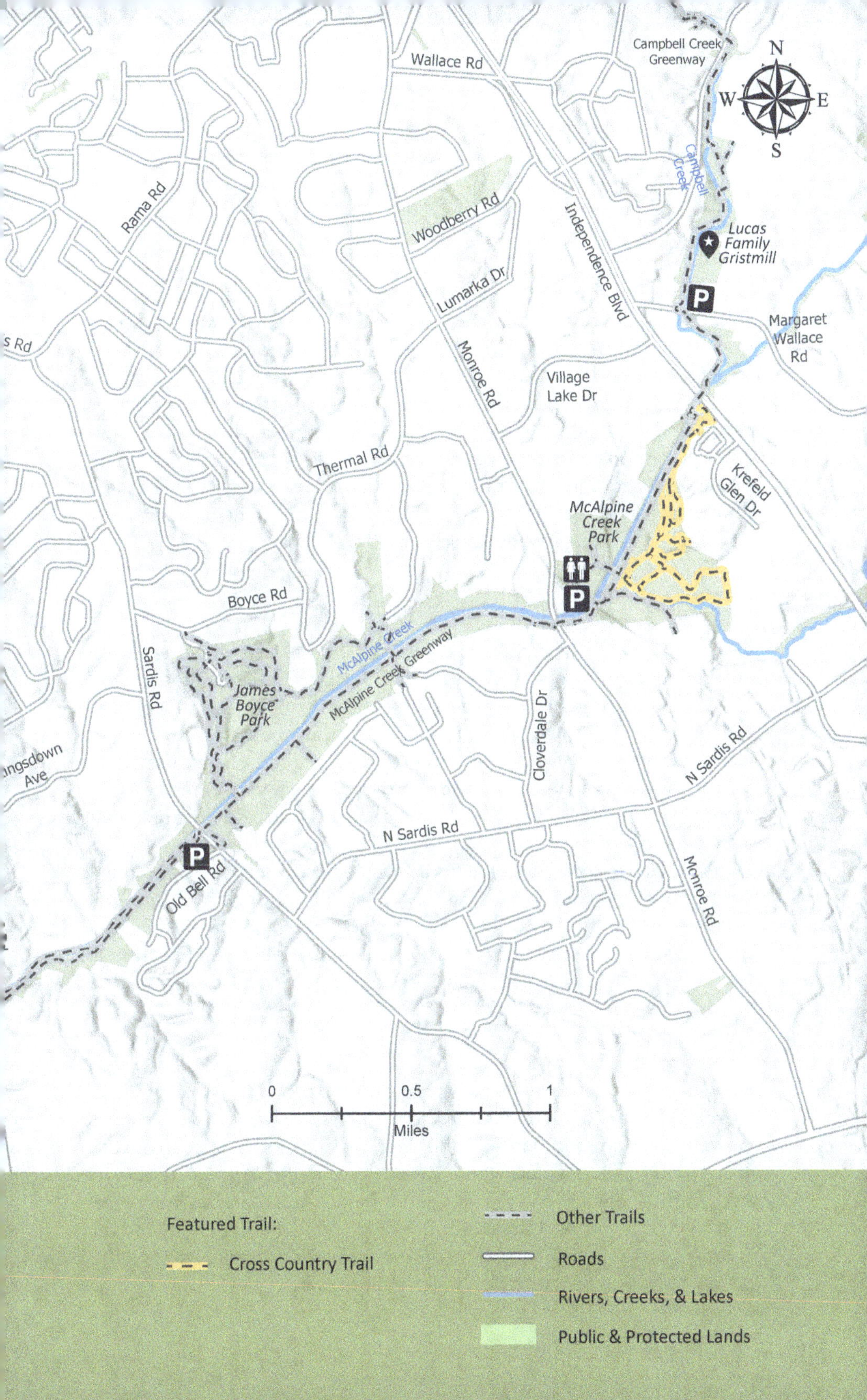

Wallace Rd
Campbell Creek Greenway
N
W
E
S
Rama Rd
Woodberry Rd
Lumarka Dr
Independence Blvd
Campbell Creek
Lucas Family Gristmill
P
Margaret Wallace Rd
s Rd
Monroe Rd
Village Lake Dr
Krefeld Glen Dr
Thermal Rd
McAlpine Creek Park
P
Boyce Rd
McAlpine Creek
McAlpine Creek Greenway
Sardis Rd
James Boyce Park
Cloverdale Dr
N Sardis Rd
ngsdown Ave
Old Bell Rd
P
N Sardis Rd
Monroe Rd
0
0.5
1
Miles
Featured Trail:
Cross Country Trail
Other Trails
Roads
Rivers, Creeks, & Lakes
Public & Protected Lands

which has been serving Matthews since 1900. Specializing in gardening, local agricultural products (even baby chicks!), and hard-to-find tools and supplies, Renfrow's offers a true old school experience.

Brakeman's Coffee & Supply
225 N. Trade St., Matthews, NC 28105

Named after a railroad brakeman whose job is to make passengers feel comfortable and safe by regulating train speeds, Brakeman's wants you to slow down and enjoy a delicious, handcrafted cup of coffee, designed to be "beautiful, tasteful, creative, fun, and inspiring." Located in a renovated, historic, white cottage, the decor is comfortable and cozy, with a variety of indoor and outdoor seating, including a patio nestled inside a white picket fence. Brakeman's serves classic and signature coffee drinks, as well as teas, shakes, and smoothies. Don't forget hot chocolate and horchata are options for kids or adults. After your busy morning or day, do as they say: "Take it slow. Do it well. Bring friends along." Closed on Sunday.

Carolina Beer Temple + The Local Scoop
195 N. Trade St., Matthews, NC 28105

Originally a post office, this unique space now houses a craft beer bar. Owners Rob and Megan Jacik opened Carolina Beer Temple to celebrate the spirit of fresh, quality, local beers. They specialize in beers made in North Carolina by independently owned breweries, truly embracing the state's vast local craft brew network. Also included on their menu are some hard ciders and seltzers, as well as nonalcoholic beers. After you select your beverage, find a table inside by the bar, bask outside in the sun at a picnic table, or pop under a shade umbrella, and relax. If inspired, take on your friends in a game of cornhole. Play to see who buys ice cream at The Local Scoop, located behind Carolina Beer Temple. The Local Scoop is all about sourcing fresh ingredients from regional farms. They offer plenty of flavors to tempt your taste buds such as sea salted caramel, honey vanilla, and coffee toffee. Just FYI, there are two other Local Scoop locations in Charlotte for more cold, creamy treats!

The Exchange Pizza Depot
213 N. Trade St., Ste. B, Matthews, NC 28105

Now that you have worked up an appetite at the park, The Exchange Pizza Depot can come to the rescue! Tucked back into the side patio of Seaboard Brewery, Taproom, and Wine Bar, this delicious pizza joint serves Neapolitan-style pizzas sure to please anyone. Choose a signature pie or create your own from a list of toppings and sauces. Gluten-free crust is available. Want more veggies in your life? Add a salad to your order. A handful of other "Odds and Ends" are available, too, such as quesadillas and grilled cheese. Relax on the patio with your order and a beverage from Seaboard.

Charlotte Rail Trail

Distance: **7 miles, round trip, out and back**
Difficulty Level: **easy**
Trailhead: **on-street parking or parking garages in South End**

Jobs fill your pockets, but adventures fill your soul.
— *Jaime Lyn Beatty*

Looking for a uniquely urban trail experience? Be sure to put the Charlotte Rail Trail on your list! Currently 3.5 miles long, this paved path connects the Queen City's South End to Uptown, taking advantage of a comfortable space alongside the LYNX Blue Line light rail. The trail delights visitors with creative art installations and provides "front-door" access to a varied collection of restaurants, shops, breweries, and gathering spots. Smooth and well-maintained, the trail is plenty wide to accommodate runners, cyclists, commuters, dog walkers, and amblers.

The art displays, both permanent and temporary, include giant yellow porch swings, where you will want to stop for a spell; a dinosaur statue; metal roosters; a giant interactive chalkboard, where passersby scrawl answers to prompts; murals; the Color Forest; and a magic carpet. But wait, that's not all! There is a permanent Ping-Pong table, picnic tables, eclectic benches, and solar charging stations, not to mention amazing skyline views. There's even a bike pump station and dog-friendly amenities. Come visit this linear, urban playground and public commons with friends or family and enjoy the day. Bring your own wheels, or rent an electric scooter from a ride-sharing program like Bird, Lime, or Spin, or an electric bike from Charlotte Joy Rides (the first bike share system in North Carolina).

More to Know

In the mid-1990s, this corridor was home to a refurbished vintage trolley line, running between Uptown and South End, generating tourism for the city center. While Charlotte managers were planning for the line, the trail space itself was created out of the requirement for an emergency vehicle pathway. Eventually, the growing city had a need for a more efficient people mover, and the high-speed transit system, named the Blue Line, replaced the trolleys, with its first phase opening in 2007.

Charlotte's Blue Line was originally designed to expand transportation options with a series of rapid transit stations. Planners realized that the space alongside the rail line offered a unique opportunity to create something special: a vibrant public recreation amenity that connects multiple neighborhoods and residential complexes with access to restaurants and businesses. The long-term plan is for the trail to extend 11 miles, from Sugar Creek Station in the north to Arrowood Station in the south. There are a few gaps remaining, most notably an $11 million project to build a stunning pedestrian bridge across I-277.

Running Thoughts

This is a popular trail, especially on weekends, so be prepared for the urban hustle bustle, with many dog walkers, cyclists, and transit riders. The art along the route is quite a highlight, either to view as you pass or to stop and interact. If you like group runs, check online with one of the many Charlotte running groups, such as the Barn Burners Run Club, which meets up for a weekly group run along the trail. It's always nice to exercise with others, meet new people, and try new routes.

Getting There

There are many points of access and areas for parking in Charlotte's South End. But if you want to experience the full trail, consider parking on neighborhood streets by the Carson Station (218 E. Carson Blvd.) just south of Uptown. You can also commute to the trail on the light rail train and exit at any station in the South End. For schedules and more information: charlottenc.gov/CATS/Rail. Bikes are permitted on the trains. There are no public restrooms along the trail.

Extend Your Trip

Pair your Rail Trail outing with a visit to Uptown, where there are numerous museums, art galleries, performance centers, restaurants, shopping areas, and big-time sports venues. The Charlotte area has an extensive 70-mile greenway system. Currently, the longest is Little Sugar Creek Greenway, a beautifully maintained urban trail that goes all the way to the South Carolina border (15 miles one way, with a few gaps). The Cross Charlotte Trail, when complete, will total 30 miles, extending from City of Pineville to the Cabarrus County line crossing through Uptown and the UNC Charlotte campus.

Hungry? Let's Eat!

Two Scoops Creamery (South End)
1616 Camden Rd. #100, Charlotte, NC 28203

Opened by three best friends in 2016, this creamery is only a block from the Rail Trail, serves unique flavors with clever names, and offers a variety of toppings to consider. Or create a milkshake from any of their many flavors (100 throughout the year, on a seasonal/rotating basis). Try their Red Velvet Cake, Not Your Mama's Pumpkin Pie, Reindeer Tracks, S'Mores, or maybe the Slow Poke, if that is your speed. They even have a selection of vegan options. Check out more flavors on their website at twoscoopscreamery.com. Their award-winning ice cream can also be found in four other locations in Charlotte and surrounding towns, with the original being the Plaza Midwood neighborhood shop. South End location open Thursday through Sunday.

Futo Buta Ramen House
222 E. Bland St., Charlotte, NC 28203

Noodle bowls are not something you find traditionally in the South, but this Charlotte restaurant's authentic Japanese menu "displays a true homage to the history of ramen as a regionalized dish," says chef and founder Michael Shortino. Futo Buta sources local pork and serves dishes in handmade pottery crafted right here in North Carolina. Their ramen bowls are plentiful, loaded with flavor, and very satisfying any time of year. Or try their organic mushroom and tofu gyoza, roasted beets and organic greens, or fried brussels sprouts, and pair your meal with one of many sake drinks on the menu. Located directly on the Rail Trail, the small shop has cozy tables, bar-height tables, and bar seating, as well as an outdoor patio. Futo Buta rocks (as does their music) and has a second location in downtown Asheville, should you find yourself there. Closed on Tuesday.

Trolley Barn Fermentory and Food Hall
2104 South Blvd., Charlotte, NC 28203

Uniquely crafted beers, creative cocktails, and a delicious selection of lunch, brunch, and dinner items await you at Trolley Barn. Located adjacent to the Rail Trail at Atherton Mill, this brewery, taproom, and three individually branded food stalls (each with their own menus created by award-winning chef Gene Briggs) are all under one roof. Delight your taste buds with duck carnitas tacos, a chorizo and egg breakfast burrito, grilled chicken gyro, bison chili, charcuterie, handmade pretzels, and so much more. All food stations can be ordered through your table or at the bar. After a day of art and exercise on this urban trail, it's a treat to hang out in Trolley Barn's two-story patio space (which is very pet-friendly), or grab a seat in the taproom. Visit trolleybarnclt.com for menu and hours. The Barn Burners Run Club meets here on Mondays.

Trail Tip: Urban trails can be busy. Keep an eye out for others, and be aware of different types of trail users who move at different speeds, especially cyclists.

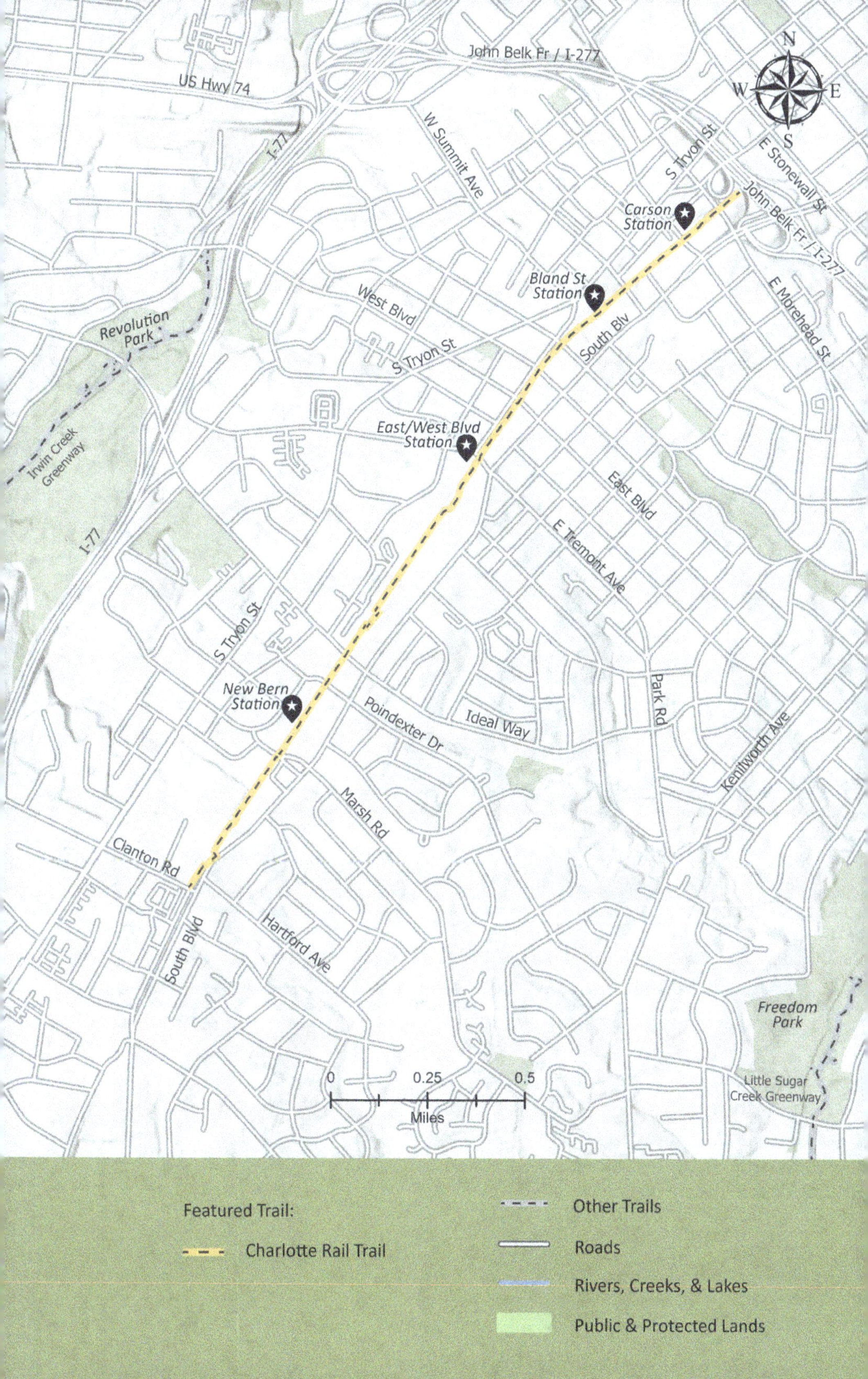

John Belk Fr / I-277
US Hwy 74
W Summit Ave
S Tryon St
E Stonewall St
Carson Station
Bland St Station
South Blv
E Morehead St
West Blvd
S Tryon St
Revolution Park
Irwin Creek Greenway
I-77
East/West Blvd Station
East Blvd
E Tremont Ave
New Bern Station
S Tryon St
Poindexter Dr
Ideal Way
Park Rd
Kenilworth Ave
Marsh Rd
Clanton Rd
South Blvd
Hartford Ave
Freedom Park
Little Sugar Creek Greenway
John Belk Fr / I-277
0   0.25   0.5
Miles
Featured Trail:
Charlotte Rail Trail
Other Trails
Roads
Rivers, Creeks, & Lakes
Public & Protected Lands
N
W   E
S

Latta Nature Preserve

Distance: **3.5 miles, lollipop loop, with extension options**
Difficulty Level: **moderate**
Trailhead: **6345 Sample Rd., Huntersville, NC 28078**

Heaven is under our feet as well as over our heads.
— Henry David Thoreau

Latta Nature Preserve, encompassing 1,460 acres, is a perfect place for an all-day outdoor adventure. The preserve features 16 miles of hiking, running, and equestrian trails, which show off the peaceful forest and lakeshore, picnic shelters, a fishing dock, and two canoe/kayak launches. It also features Quest, a recently constructed, not-to-miss nature center. Interesting and engaging at any age, Quest houses interactive displays about freshwater and natural habitats in the region.

The preserve has many different trails and routes to choose from. Our recommended trail combination departs from the nature center on the Hill Trail, connects to the Forest Loop, then follows the Split Rock Trail along the lakeshore, and returns to the parking area on the Hill Trail for a total of approximately 3.5 miles. The Hill Trail starts in the shade, then opens up into a sunny prairie. From there, connect to the Forest Loop, which will return you to a shaded canopy of scarlet and post oaks, shagbark and bitternut hickory, and shortleaf and loblolly pines. If you are up for a longer route, we suggest extending your hike/run by adding in the 1.7-mile Cove Trail to take in more of the scenic shoreline. These combined trails allow you to experience the Piedmont prairie, oak-hickory forest, and freshwater lake areas, comprising the three biomes at Latta Nature Preserve. You can learn more about biomes inside Quest.

All of the trails are clearly marked with signs using colors and shapes. We recommend taking a photo of the trail system map on your phone or carrying a hard copy of the map. Quest has a large wall map in the lobby to study and photograph before you head out.

More to Know

Charlotte ranks among the country's fastest-growing metro areas. It is expected to grow by another 50 percent by 2050, from about 3 million to 4.5 million people. Amid all this growth, Mecklenburg County has created a network of 27 nature preserves and four nature centers, strategically protecting more than 8,000 acres of forests, grasslands, wetlands, and rare species. Latta Nature Preserve is the largest and protects the endangered Schweinitz's Sunflower. Situated on Mountain Island Lake, which is fed by the Catawba River, Latta Nature Preserve helps protect the quality of drinking water for the more than one million Charlotte area residents who depend on this water source.

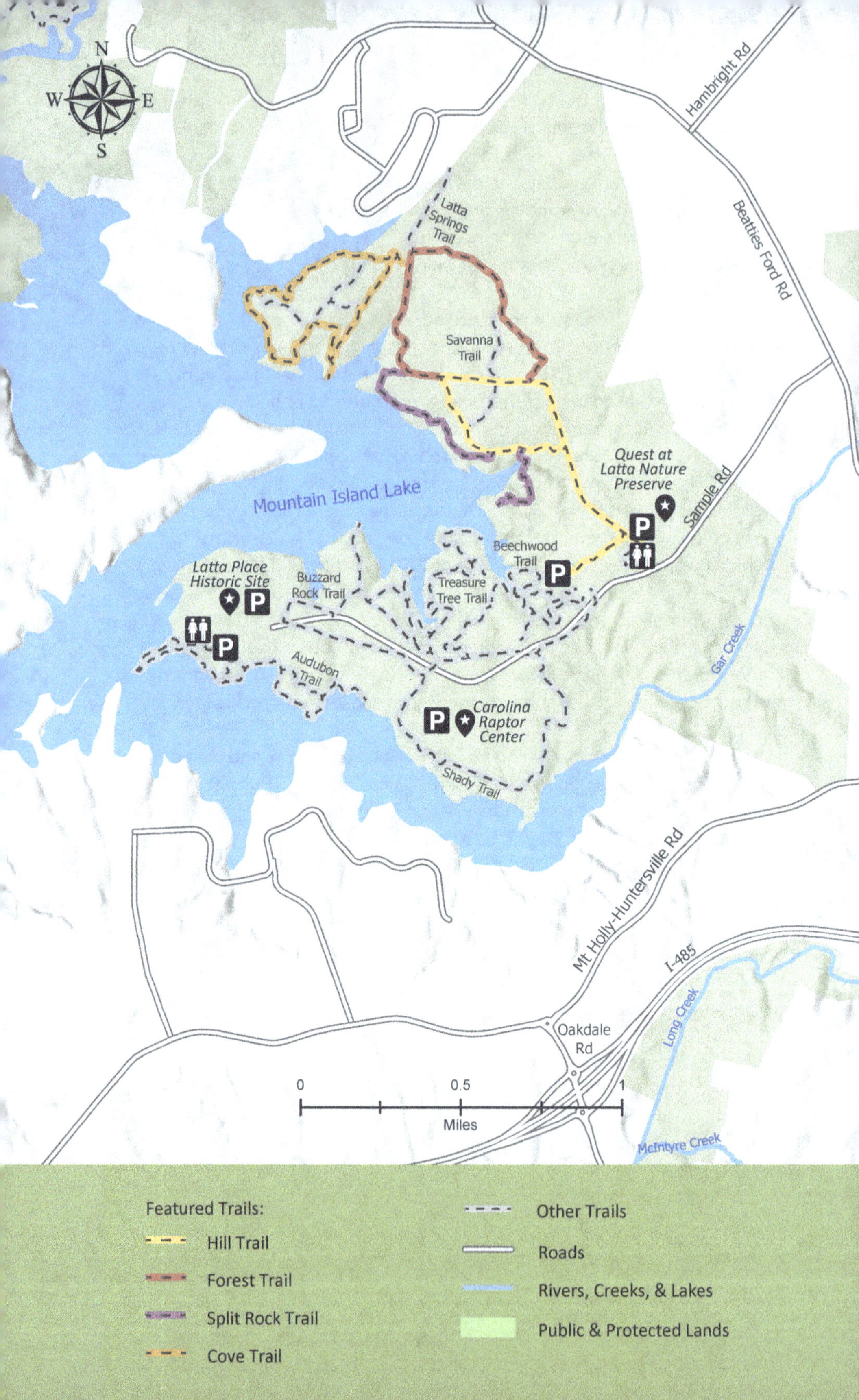

N
W E
S
Hambright Rd
Beatties Ford Rd
Latta Springs Trail
Savanna Trail
Sample Rd
Quest at Latta Nature Preserve
P
Beechwood Trail
P
Latta Place Historic Site
P
Buzzard Rock Trail
Treasure Tree Trail
P
P
Mountain Island Lake
Audubon Trail
P
Carolina Raptor Center
Shady Trail
Gar Creek
Mt Holly-Huntersville Rd
I-485
Oakdale Rd
Long Creek
McIntyre Creek
0
0.5
1
Miles
Featured Trails:
Hill Trail
Forest Trail
Split Rock Trail
Cove Trail
Other Trails
Roads
Rivers, Creeks, & Lakes
Public & Protected Lands

Running Thoughts

Latta's trails offer plentiful options for your long run, with the ease of putting together many different trail combinations in the preserve. If parking at Quest, consider carrying less in your pack and circling back past the center for a restroom break or to refill your water bottle after a few miles. Once you refuel, explore another few miles of additional trails at a comfortable long-run pace.

Getting There

Located off Beatties Ford Road, Latta Nature Preserve is close to Huntersville, just 20 minutes north of Uptown Charlotte. Low stone walls mark the turn onto Sample Road, and the entrance is clearly marked with a large, attractive sign. There's a convenient parking lot at the nature center, with clean restrooms and easy access to the trails. Additional parking is available farther into the park.

Extend Your Trip

Don't miss exploring Quest, which is free to the public and greets you as you enter the preserve. The center features live animals and a large exhibit hall, including a 6,000-gallon aquarium. "Gar," a cartoon gar fish used in the signage, will help guide you through the exhibits. Check the center's calendar for a wide variety of outdoor education and adventure programs for all ages. Some programs have a fee.

Feel like getting on the water? There are two canoe/kayak launches in quiet coves protected by a no-wake zone, safe for kids to enjoy water activities including paddleboards and tubes. Bring your own gear, or call Mountain Island Lake Paddle Co.; they deliver to Latta's launch area on Gar Creek. If fishing is more your thing, check out the fishing dock. If you don't have your own fishing rod, you can borrow one at the front desk and purchase bait in the gift shop. Individuals over the age of 16 must have a North Carolina fishing license. Want to explore the history of this land? Visit Latta Place, a

historic house built around 1800 and originally part of a 742-acre plantation. It has living history exhibits and a research center, and in-person interpretation will be available soon.

If you have the time and interest, check out the Carolina Raptor Center's .75-mile self-guided Raptor Trail, located next to Quest. It showcases more than 30 birds of prey, including eagles, falcons, owls, hawks, and many more predatory birds in their outdoor aviary. The center offers a wide range of programs and operates a medical center assisting 800–1,000 injured birds each year. Note: there is an entrance fee for the Raptor Trail.

Hungry? Let's Eat!

If you packed a lunch or snack, there are plenty of picnic tables and shelters in the nature preserve or try one of these options below.

Pinky's Westside Grill
9818 Gilead Rd. Ste. 101B, Huntersville, NC 28078

If you are looking for a rollicking spot with unique decor, Pinky's is your place. Chef Greg Auten has a long culinary history in the Charlotte area and perfected the diner when he and his partner, Andy Cauble, opened Pinky's more than a decade ago. Ready to serve you any day of the week, the staff, food, location, drinks, and outright charm will have you coming back again and again. They offer a variety of American favorites, from "Undisputed Heavy-weight Championship Burgers" and hot dogs under the menu heading "Walking in a Weiner Wonderland," to a section of "Not Just for Tuesday Tacos." All menu categories have meat and vegetarian options. Give Greg's appetizers a try. Perhaps you'll like his namesake fried pickles, or maybe the Pimp'n Fries, consisting of their "world-famous homemade pimento cheese melted over waffle fries," to curb your post-trail hunger. If you still have room, try their banana "Nan'er" pudding. Featured on *Diners, Drive-Ins and Dives,* this hot spot is sure to please. In the episode, Guy Fieri lets out the best-kept secret on the menu, the green chili pork. Check out Pinky's original location in Charlotte.

Lancaster's BBQ
9230 Beatties Ford Rd., Huntersville, NC 28078

Are you craving barbecue? Lancaster's is a perfect refueling station after your hike or run, offering melt-in-your-mouth barbecue, warm hush puppies, and choices of many traditional Southern sides. Jeff Lancaster's slow-smoked, eastern NC-style barbecue has fed countless families, sports legends, and other famous patrons for nearly three decades. Closed on Monday, this location of Lancaster's BBQ was established in 2006 in the historic Puckett's Gas Station and General Store. Its family-fun atmosphere and dedicated staff aim to please. Visit the original Lancaster's in Mooresville, established in 1986.

SUNRISE EGG CUPS

If you don't have time for a sit-down, hot breakfast as you head out the door for your day's adventure, a precooked egg cup is the just the answer. These are easy and can be made ahead of time and kept in the fridge for a few days or frozen. Pop them in the microwave or toaster oven to warm them up, and a healthy, protein-packed breakfast is served!

INGREDIENTS:

5 eggs
2 tablespoons milk
grated or crumbled cheese
(feta, cheddar, or
your favorite cheese)
cooked and crumbled bacon
or sausage, if desired
finely chopped veggies of
your choice, uncooked
(onions, peppers,
mushrooms, spinach)
salt and pepper to taste

DIRECTIONS:

Preheat oven to 350°F. Spray/grease muffin tin. In a large bowl, beat eggs well and add milk. Add salt and pepper to taste. In a separate bowl, mix desired combination of meat and veggies, then add to each egg cup, filling 2/3 of the way. Pour egg mixture into each cup, filling to the top. Sprinkle the cheese on top, or as a layer on the bottom if you choose. Bake for 20 minutes, or until the top is set. Serve them hot or save for later. Yields 6–8 egg cups.

Duke Kimbrell Trail, Seven Oaks Preserve

Distance: **5.2 miles, round trip, out and back, or 5 miles, loop**
Difficulty Level: **easy**
Trailhead: **6900 S. New Hope Rd., Belmont, NC 28012**

The woods are lovely, dark and deep.
But I have promises to keep,
and miles to go before I sleep.
— Robert Frost

This natural surface trail at Seven Oaks Preserve meanders along the shoreline of Lake Wylie through a mostly shaded forest with several creek crossings. Open to biking and hiking, the trail is located on 78 acres of preserved land managed by the Catawba Lands Conservancy. The Duke Kimbrell Trail is an out-and-back format. However, you can create a 5-mile loop by using connector trails around the Daniel Stowe Botanical Garden. To follow the loop option, look for the Persimmon Trail sign about 1 mile from the New Hope Trailhead, and follow it to the Botanical Garden parking lot. Then continue along the back side of the parking lot to the Worrell's Walk Trail, which connects back to the Duke Kimbrell Trail to finish the loop. Mountain bikes are allowed on the Duke Kimbrell Trail except during wet conditions and are not allowed on the Daniel Stowe Botanical Garden's trails. While there is a fee to enter the Garden, trail users do not have to pay the fee to use the Persimmon and Worrell's Walk trails.

More to Know

The Duke Kimbrell Trail is part of the Carolina Thread Trail, a planned regional network of greenways, trails, and blueways (paddle trails) connecting 15 counties in the Charlotte area. With a goal of 1,600 trail miles, there are currently more than 300 miles of trails and 170 miles of blueway open to the public in the Carolina Thread Trail network. See carolinathreadtrail.org for more information and trail ideas in the network.

Seven Oaks Preserve protects an important natural shore area around Lake Wylie for wildlife habitat and clean water. In the spring, the beautiful and fragrant native blooming snowbell may catch your eye. Look for the unusually large swamp chestnut oak trees along the lake's edge. These trees were once used to make farm baskets, and they produce large acorns that are an important food for many animals. The preserve also supports very large tulip trees, pawpaws, and persimmon trees. If you are lucky, you may see ospreys, eagles, or kingfishers soaring over the water.

Running Thoughts

This trail is flat and wide enough to run next to a running companion (human or furry friend), staying mindful of other trail users going and coming. You can make this an easy out-and-back run along the water's edge, enjoying shade the majority of the trail's length. Or take the detour and complete the loop using the Daniel Stowe Botanical Garden's trails. Either way, it's generally easy footing without many roots, rocks, or inclines, making it a good choice for first-time trail runners. If you are looking to challenge yourself a bit partway through your run, throw in pace pickups for about 60 seconds every 5 minutes or so. (Pickups are faster-paced segments added into an easy or moderate run.)

Getting There

Located within 0.5 miles of the South Carolina border, Seven Oaks Preserve is southwest of Charlotte and very close to the quaint towns of Cramerton, Belmont, and McAdenville. The gravel parking lot for the Duke Kimbrell Trail is marked with a sign, but keep a lookout or you may drive past it. There are no restrooms at the trailhead, but there are restrooms at the Daniel Stowe Botanical Garden's Visitor Pavilion during open hours, located at 6500 S. New Hope Road.

Extend Your Trip

Complete your day with a visit to the adjacent Daniel Stowe Botanical Garden which has 30 acres of magnificent grounds to explore, including a children's garden, a conservatory with tropical plants and orchids, a Dry Piedmont Prairie, annual and perennial displays, sparkling fountains, and a gorgeous Visitor Pavilion. In the warmer months, the Butterfly Bungalow is fun for kids and adults alike. Their online calendar lists yoga, art, and photography classes, as well as other special events.

While in the area, consider a visit to Belmont, Cramerton, or McAdenville, where you can find a number of places to grab a bite to eat or drink. Cramerton features Goat Island Park, a small park in the middle of the South Fork Catawba River accessed by one of the Goat Island Greenway pedestrian bridges or by kayak. The park features an observation pier, picnic shelters, a natural treehouse-style playground, an 18-hole disc golf course, permanent Ping-Pong tables and cornhole boards, and a short greenway.

On Belmont's Main Street, you will find historic charm with small shops and local eateries, watering holes, and greenspace at Stowe Park, which is part of the Carolina Thread Trail and has a playground for kids.

McAdenville is most famous for its Christmas Town USA lights display. It's one of the largest holiday lights shows in the country, attracting people from all over.

Trail Tip: *Pack it out. Keep extra plastic bags handy on your hike for waste, including pet waste, or other trash you might spot along the trail. Don't throw that banana or orange peel into the woods. They take two years to decompose!*

N
W E
S
S New Hope Rd
Worrells River Rd
P
P
Persimmon Trail
Daniel Stowe Botanical Gardens
Worrells Walk
Lake Wylie
Armstrong Rd
S New Hope Rd
New Hope Rd Trailhead
P
Catawba Cove Dr
North Carolina
South Carolina
0
0.25
0.5
Miles
Featured Trail:
Duke Kimbrell Trail at Seven Oaks Preserve
State Boundary
Other Trails
Roads
Rivers, Creeks, & Lakes
Public & Protected Lands

Hungry? Let's Eat!

Daniel Stowe Botanical Garden
6500 S. New Hope Rd., Belmont, NC 28012

Daniel Stowe Botanical Garden has a spectacular lawn and some patio tables for your picnic. If you are planning to pay the entrance fee, bring your lunch and relax in their manicured gardens after a day on the trails. You can also stop by The Garden Store & Wine Nook (within the Visitor Pavilion) where you can purchase cold drinks and light snacks such as nuts, chips, and crackers. The Garden is closed on Monday and Tuesday. Also note a new trailhead store is open, offering coffee, beer, wine, and light foods, and provides access to some trails without the entrance fee to the formal gardens. Check online for hours.

Floyd & Blackie's Coffee House, Ice Cream & Blossom Bakery
142 8th Ave., Cramerton, NC 28032

Floyd & Blackie's can energize your day with their full-service coffee bar, or satisfy your sweet tooth with made-from-scratch bakery items and an array of Hershey's Ice Cream flavors. The bakery also serves a delicious breakfast, lunch, or dinner. The menu has a wide variety of appealing pre- or post-trail eats. Their location across from Goat Island Park means you can easily work off your renewed energy. There is also a Floyd & Blackie's (bakery items only) in McAdenville, serving cookies, cakes, and other sweet treats.

Spruced Goose Station
118 Wesleyan Dr., McAdenville, NC 28101

This lovely café offers friendly service and an extensive menu, with morning favorites, light options, sandwiches, flatbreads, hot dogs, wraps, salads, and soups, as well as a full coffee menu. There are plenty of sweet treats available, too. They serve local Mooresville Ice Cream (which was started way back in 1924!), banana splits, shakes, cakes, muffins, cookies, brownies, and more. Dine with your selections in the comfortable interior space or outside on the front patio. Spruced Goose Station, closed on Sunday, offers mean-ingful employment for people with disabilities; it is one of four businesses established by Holy Angels. Check out Cotton Candy Factory, Cherubs Café, and Bliss Gallery in Belmont, all operating with the same mission.

Pinnacle Trail, Crowders Mountain State Park

Distance: **4.5 miles, loop**
Difficulty Level: **moderate**
Trailhead: **522 Park Office Ln., Kings Mountain, NC 28086**

Between every two pines there is a doorway to a new world.
— *John Muir*

Crowders Mountain State Park is the most well-known hiking destination in the Charlotte area. With its unique craggy peaks, towering cliffs, and magnificent views of the Charlotte skyline and surrounding region, it's worth the trip from other areas of the state. The hike we are featuring creates a loop from the visitor center with a climb to the highest peak in Gaston County: the 1,705-foot Pinnacle. The newly improved trail is mostly wide and smooth but gains about 800 feet in elevation, making the hike moderately difficult. At the top you will find a maze of narrow trails and rocks to navigate, with views that will take your breath away.

The visitor center has restrooms, picnic tables, water fountains, and a small museum featuring the plants and animals found in the park. There is also an interactive sandbox where you can create mountains and rivers with your hands, a fun activity for all ages.

After your hike up to the Pinnacle, take your picnic to one of the many picnic shelters nearby. But don't miss the Lake Trail! Only 0.8 miles long, this exceptionally scenic and mostly flat trail meanders through the woods at the edge of a small lake, delighting all with ducks, turtles sunning on logs, and maybe even a great blue heron looking for its next meal.

More to Know

The peaks of Crowders Mountain are part of the Appalachian chain that formed 450 to 500 million years ago. Made of quartzite, these remnant pinnacles have withstood the eroding forces of wind and water, and once marked the boundaries between hunting lands for the Cherokee and Catawba Indians.

Crowders Mountain State Park was formed in 1973 following a successful local grassroots effort to protect the land after a private company started the process to purchase mineral rights. Today, Crowders Mountain State Park connects to Kings Mountain State Park and Kings Mountain National Military Park in South Carolina via the 6.2-mile Ridgeline Trail.

Running Thoughts

The Lake Trail, which encircles the water with a crushed gravel path and is marked with blue blazes, is perfect for a multiple-lap workout. Half-mile repeats might be a good choice here, jogging the remainder of the 0.8-mile loop for the recovery between 800s. Or, if you are looking for a long-run route with some challenging ups and downs, choose to connect the Pinnacle Trail to the Ridgeline Trail. Ridgeline will give you up to an additional 12.4 miles round trip, and then you can say you've run to South Carolina and back!

Getting There

Crowders Mountain State Park is located just off I-85, 30 miles west of Charlotte and close to Kings Mountain. There are three access points: Linwood Road, Sparrow Springs, and Boulders. Our featured trail starts at the Sparrow Springs Access, which has the park's only visitor center. There are restrooms and water fountains at the visitor center.

Extend Your Trip

If you want to get in more miles and haven't had enough of the stunning views, follow the 2.8-mile Crowders Trail from the Sparrow Springs Visitor Center across Sparrow Springs Road to get to the top of the park's namesake, Crowders Mountain. Or if you plan to go into Kings Mountain, take a side trip to the Kings Mountain Gateway Trails, where you will find a network of 6.4 miles of trails, including a rail trail, hill climbs, and scenic views of Crowders Mountain.

Trail Tip: *Timing is everything. If you choose a popular trail, plan your hike or run in the middle of the week or on an early morning. Weekends tend to be very crowded and less relaxing.*

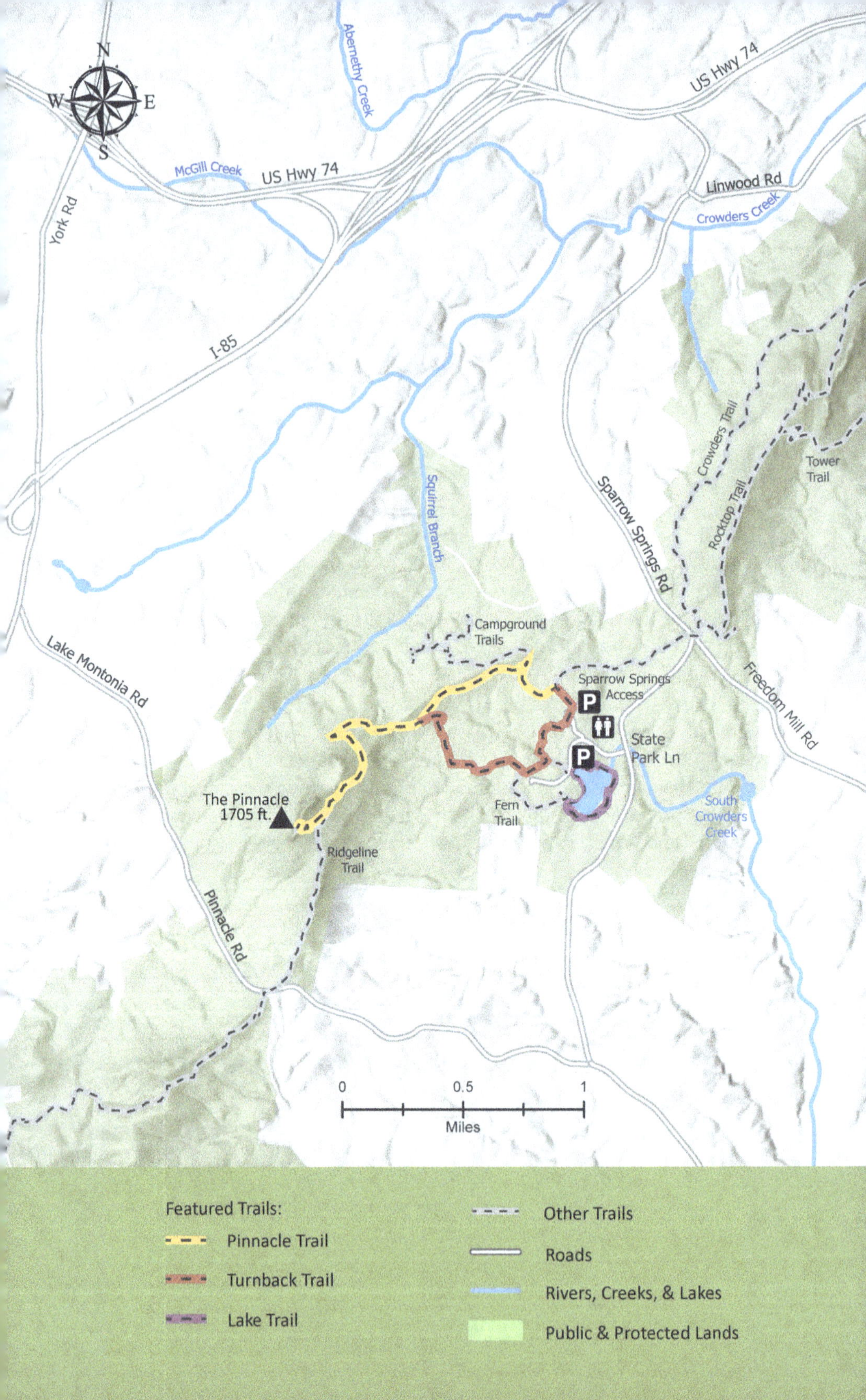

N
W E
S
Abernethy Creek
US Hwy 74
Linwood Rd
McGill Creek
US Hwy 74
Crowders Creek
York Rd
I-85
Sparrow Springs Rd
Crowders Trail
Rocktop Trail
Tower Trail
Squirrel Branch
Lake Montonia Rd
Campground Trails
Sparrow Springs Access
P
P
State Park Ln
Freedom Mill Rd
The Pinnacle 1705 ft.
Fern Trail
South Crowders Creek
Ridgeline Trail
Pinnacle Rd
0
0.5
1
Miles
Featured Trails:
Pinnacle Trail
Turnback Trail
Lake Trail
Other Trails
Roads
Rivers, Creeks, & Lakes
Public & Protected Lands

Hungry? Let's Eat!

Big Red's Cafe

830 E. King St., Kings Mountain, NC 28086

Big Red's Cafe is a charming stop for a bite to eat after hitting the trails, with its inviting rocking chairs on the wraparound porch, or inside, at a cozy table or sofa area. There's something for everyone: cold and hot coffees; lattes and frappés; ice cream, smoothies, and fresh lemonades; sammies, salads and sides; or breakfast all day (sausage, egg and cheese on a waffle, please!), or choose a warmed-up baked good.

Pita Wheel

110 S. York St., Gastonia, NC 28052

Pita Wheel began as a food truck in 2014, and today it has grown into a full-service, dine-in restaurant located in downtown Gastonia. With its towering Sinclair Dino sign, vintage style, bold colors, and retro murals inside,

you can't miss it. In pleasant weather, the patio is a great place to enjoy a drink or meal. Family- and dog-friendly, you are going to dig their epic vibe in the converted corner gas station. Pita Wheel's staff will be happy to take your order and curb your off-the-trail hunger with burgers, Phillys, pitas, wraps, salads, and sides such as fried pickles and baked mac and cheese. The bar offers cocktails, a host of draft beers, and a small selection of wines. Catch local, live music on certain days of the week. Visit the music schedule online at pitawheel.com. Check out the two other locations in nearby Dallas and Belmont.

Bakers Mountain Park

Distance: **2.5 miles, loop**
Difficulty Level: **moderate**
Trailhead: **6680 Bakers Mountain Rd., Hickory, NC 28602**

To walk in nature is to witness a thousand miracles.
— Marie Davis

The Bakers Mountain Loop Trail climbs to the top of Bakers Mountain, the highest point in Catawba County (elevation 1,780 feet), offering expansive views of the Catawba Valley and distant mountains from an observation deck. On a clear day, look for Grandfather Mountain and Mount Mitchell. The trail is steep and rooty in sections going up to the top and coming back down, but it's worth it for the views. The section of the trail along the creek

is lovely, with multiple points to access the clear water. It includes a small but scenic waterfall. We recommend following the loop in a counterclockwise direction by looking for the start of the trail on the right side of the park office/restroom. The trails are clearly marked. There are several other trails and connectors you can follow in the park to lengthen your visit. The restroom/parking area is nicely landscaped, and it has a stack of hiking sticks to borrow, a water bowl for pups, and a large picnic shelter.

More to Know

Long before becoming a park, Bakers Mountain was a popular place for gatherings, including church outings and religious pilgrimages, and for local youth to explore. Named after the Baker family, who settled the land in the late 1700s, the mountain hid Tories during the Revolutionary War. Today, the park covers 189 acres of mature Chestnut Oak forest with nearly 6 miles of trails. During your visit, look for wildlife and plants native to the North Carolina mountains. The park has a 0.25-mile paved path circling the parking lot, with 18 stations featuring informative panels based on children's books, called a LITeracy Trail (LIT = literature, information, and technology).

Running Thoughts

Pack your water and set out on a gentle run in the woods with a running buddy. This is a great place to run at a talking pace. After the steep climb up, catch your breath with a stellar view at the observation platform and gazebo (and a little sip of that water you brought along). Most of the Bakers Mountain trails are well shaded and wide enough to run side-by-side. On flatter areas along the creek, pick up your pace as desired. Or run a first lap easy, and do it again at a faster pace, making it a 5-mile run. The park office/restroom/parking area has a small flat lawn to stretch and have a snack when you finish.

Trail Tip: *Don't disturb nature. Take only pictures. Leave what you find so others can enjoy the same beauty and awe.*

Getting There

Bakers Mountain Park is a short distance from Exit 121 off I-40 and is easy to find. Follow signs on Old Shelby Road to Bakers Mountain Road where you will find a clearly marked sign at the park entrance. The parking lot may get busy on weekends, but there is overflow parking on the road.

Extend Your Trip

Catawba County has four excellent parks, all featuring trails. The newest is Mountain Creek Park, on the northwest shores of Lake Norman. Mountain Creek Park has a very large adventure playground, 19 miles of mountain bike trails, pickleball courts, a dog park, a fishing pier, and a canoe/kayak launch. Riverbend Park also features nearly 20 miles of trails.

Hungry? Let's Eat!

Recently revitalized downtown Hickory is vibrant, quaint, and walkable. It has ample parking, outdoor seating, and a creative play space for children in the public square. The new social district allows visitors to enjoy beverages while exploring the downtown area, including a section of the scenic City Walk alongside the rail line. The City Walk connects Lenoir Rhyne University to several other greenways in Hickory, including the Art Walk, River Walk, and Aviation Walk.

Hatch Sandwich Bar
268 1st Ave. N.W., Hickory, NC 28601

Hatch Sandwich Bar offers a wide variety of homemade hot and cold sandwiches, featuring a modern twist on traditional favorites, including a pork belly BLT or a pulled pork grilled cheese. Standard deli sandwiches and vegetarian options are on the menu, too, as well as creative daily sides such as roasted cauliflower, brussels sprouts with maple syrup, and miso broccoli. Near the front counter, there is a wall of refrigerated beverages and local craft brews to pair with your lunch order. They offer a large, colorful indoor space as well as outdoor patio seating. Closed on Sunday and Monday.

N
W E
S
R H Rd
Henry River Rd
Old Shelby Rd
Old Shelby Rd
Bakers Mountain Rd
Mountain Grove Rd
Observation Platform
Bakers Mountain 1780 ft.
P
0
0.25
0.5
Miles
Featured Trail:
Bakers Mountain Loop Trail
Other Trails
Roads
Rivers, Creeks, & Lakes
Public & Protected Lands

Taste Full Beans
29 2nd St. N.W., Hickory, NC 28601

We loved the whimsical, artistic atmosphere and the friendly staff at Taste Full Beans, not to mention their name. Their extensive variety of lattes, teas, and smoothies is matched by an equally creative menu of breakfast and lunch options, ranging from bowls and burritos, to wraps, sandwiches, salads, and soups. Everything is scratch-made with a commitment to locally sourced ingredients. There are gluten-free, vegan, and vegetarian items offered. The café has a Little Free Library by the door, inviting you to take or leave a book. Or you can browse through their eclectic gift shop which is full of local books, jewelry, art, pottery, and everything imaginable for the coffee and tea lover. An outdoor patio as well as indoor tables with an oasis of plants in the dining area create a warm, beautiful space, which is a treat itself!

Riverbend Creamery
4391 Ritchie Rd., Lincolnton, NC 28092

If you are coming from the Charlotte area, or if you are willing to drive a little bit out of your way, consider a stop at the scenic Riverbend Creamery, located in the bend of the South Fork River, southeast of Bakers Mountain Park by about 18 miles. This fifth-generation, family-owned dairy raises grass-fed Jersey cows for the most delicious ice cream and milk you can find: "From our grass, to your glass" is their motto. If you come on a weekend in the warmer months, you can check out their walking tours, available on a first-come, first-serve basis ($5 per guest for about a 30-minute tour). Visit riverbendcreamery.com for details and plenty of incredible photos of their farm and adorable Jersey cows. Closed on Monday.

Riverbend cows grazing in a pasture at the creamery.

It is good to have an end to
journey towards, but it is the
journey that matters, in the end.

— Ursula K. Le Guin

Trail Races

While you may be very familiar with road races, there are also numerous trail races in all regions of the state that are fun for experienced trail runners as well as those new to the sport. Some events have multiple race distances, offer a relay option, or even run at night. Frequently, food, local brews, music, and unique, handmade awards are part of the festivities. Many races raise money for good causes, often supporting the trails themselves. We've created a list of trail races by region, including favorites that we have run for years, as well as others to consider. Some are on or near our featured trails in this guidebook. The chart on the opposing page shares information about the general location, time of year the event is held, and race distances that are offered. We recommend you look online for more information about each individual event. This list is only a sampling of trail races in North Carolina. Talk to other runners and ask about their favorites!

Volunteering

Whether you are a runner or hiker, consider giving back and helping out at a trail event. All races rely on volunteers to help pass out water and nutrition on the course, direct runners, help at the start and finish lines, etc. Working with other trail enthusiasts can be very rewarding. Sometimes volunteers can earn an entry to a future race by working an event, which is a nice perk for your efforts. Check event websites for volunteer information.

There is a race opportunity for everyone!

The green flag waves at the start of the Occoneechee Speedway Relay.

REGION	MONTH	DISTANCE
MOUNTAIN REGION		
Lake James Races, NEBO	APRIL	5K, 7 MILE
Black Mountain Monster, BLACK MOUNTAIN	JUNE	6 HOUR, 12 HOUR, 24 HOUR
Springmaid Splash, SPRUCE PINE	SEPTEMBER	5K, 10K
TreeTops Trail Races, HENDERSONVILLE	SEPTEMBER	1 MILE, 5K, 8.5 MILE
Shut-In Ridge Race, ASHEVILLE	NOVEMBER	17.8 MILE
Dirty Santa Trail Run, LENOIR	DECEMBER	4.6 MILE
TRIAD REGION		
Frosty 50, WINSTON-SALEM	JANUARY	5K, 12.5K, 25K, 50K & 50K RELAY
Whiskey Tango Foxtrot, GIBSONVILLE	JANUARY	5 MILE, HALF
Uwharrie Mountain Run, OPHIR	FEBRUARY	8 MILE, 20 MILE, 40 MILE
Northern Trails, GREENSBORO	MARCH	10 MILE, MARATHON
Cedarock Trail Run, BURLINGTON	APRIL	5K, 10K, HALF
Owl's Roost Rumble, GREENSBORO	APRIL	4 MILE, HALF
Moonlight Bootlegger, GREENSBORO	JULY	5K
Salem Lake Trail Race, WINSTON-SALEM	SEPTEMBER	5K, 7 MILE, 30K
Run at the Rock, BURLINGTON	DECEMBER	5K, 10K, HALF
TRIANGLE REGION		
Little River Trail Runs, ROUGEMONT	JANUARY	7K, 10 MILE
Occoneechee Speedway Relay, HILLSBOROUGH	JANUARY	20K RELAY
Occoneechee Mtn. Challenge, HILLSBOROUGH	JANUARY	10 MILE
Mountains-to-Sea Trail Challenge, RALEIGH	APRIL	12 MILE, 50K
Philosopher's Way Trail Runs, CHAPEL HILL	MAY	7K, 10 MILE
Zen Squirrel Trail Run, CHAPEL HILL	MAY	2 MILE, 5 MILE, 10 MILE
Common Rush Trail Run, NEW HILL	JULY	5 MILE, 10 MILE
Eno River Run, DURHAM	OCTOBER	6 MILE, 11 MILE
Root Rock Run, CHAPEL HILL	OCTOBER	5K, 10K, HALF
CHARLOTTE REGION		
Dog Days of Winter Jog & Walk, CHARLOTTE	FEBRUARY	1 MILE, 5K
New South Trail Marathon, CHARLOTTE	APRIL	HALF & MARATHON
River Jam Run Series, CHARLOTTE	MAY-SEPT	5K, 10K
Brew Dash, CHARLOTTE	JUNE	6K, 12K
Tread, White, and Blue, CHARLOTTE	JULY	5K (3 ROUTES)
Rocky Branch Trail Race, BELMONT	SEPTEMBER	5K, 10K, 25K, 50K & 50K RELAY
Tread Nightly, Tread Brightly, CHARLOTTE	SEPTEMBER	4 MILE, HALF
A Shot in the Dark, CHARLOTTE	NOVEMBER	5K, 10K, HALF

Acknowledgments

We first started talking about collaborating to produce a trail guide that combined trails with great eateries nearby back in 2021. It was a passion project, driven by our collective love of outdoor adventures and rewarding treats. Neither one of us had ever thought about writing and publishing a book. We knew we had a lot to learn, but we also realized that with Hollis' graphic design skills and running experience, and Palmer's trail expertise and involvement in the field, we would make a great team. We thought it would take a year or so and that the timing was perfect, with the approach of 2023 NC Year of the Trail, a campaign that Palmer was leading. Well, life happens. Besides our work and many volunteer commitments, we were both parenting teenagers, and one by one, getting them off to college. And then there is the cycle of life. We have enjoyed family celebrations and endured sad losses. We have experienced it all along this journey. To get here has taken much longer than we expected, but good things come to those who are patient. We had an amazing time exploring new trails and old favorites, tasting treats and working with an incredible group of friends along the way. We are truly grateful to the many who have lent a hand in creating *Trails & Treats* and those who have encouraged us on this journey.

First and foremost, we acknowledge our parents, Gay and Norman Smith, and Billie and Jef Morgan, who fostered our love for being active in the outdoors since we were young. Sharing their wisdom and their appreciation for nature provided inspiration that has shaped our lives in the most meaningful of ways. They instilled values we have worked to pass on to our own children.

Additional Acknowledgments

Thanks to Scott Pope (Scott Pope Photography) for our cover image, website design, and headshots for our web page and the book; Dr. Karen Kesler for creating our beautiful and detailed trail maps (while completing her PhD); Drew Perry for writing our foreword; Jef Morgan for the generous use of office space for the production of the book; Amelia Cook and Abby Draut for social media planning and guidance; Alice Saunders for carefully reviewing our website, book layout, and proof; Judy Carrasco for her skillful copy editing; Mary Herbenick, Mimi O'Grady, and Richard and Libby Smith for proofreading, Ellen Bradley for her review of our sample chapter and original book proposal; Bret Baronak, Bill Blackley, Vivian Coleman, David Craft, Dave Fouts, Brianna Haferman, Beth Heile, Ann Lynch, Mary Joan Pugh, and Smith Raynor for trail and treat inspirations and recommendations; Joan Nesbit Mabe for historical reference and information about the cross country trail at McAlpine Creek Park; Travis Hicks for helping us understand the world of self-publishing; Margie Satinsky and Marlie Wasserman for early inspiration and information about book publishing; Brian Lampkin and Steve Mitchell (Scuppernong Books) for publishing tips and hints; Jon Harris for helping us set up the LLC; our recipe contributors—Hollis' Uncle Spike, Caroline Cook, and Kristen Balow; our recipe testers—Nadja Cech, Kara Tate, Amy Arganbright, and Liz Tacik; Dabney Sanders (Downtown Greenway) for sharing images; and to those who helped gather trail data for our maps—Sean Bloom (Carolina Thread Trail), Nolan Carter (Alamance Parks), Erik Crews (US Forest Service), Malinda Ford (Piedmont Triad Regional Council), Elizabeth Jernigan (Greensboro Parks and Recreation), Gregory Kopsch (UNC Facilities), Brendan Moore (Durham County), Smith Raynor and John Amoroso (NC State Parks), and Hannah Royal (Triangle Land Conservancy).

To our hiking and trail running buddies who helped explore our featured trails—Amy Arganbright, Allison and Mackenzie Greiner, Mimi O'Grady, Jessica and Declan Oberlies, and Maggie, Will, and Gabby McIntyre.

Last, but absolutely not least, to our amazing husbands, JP McIntyre and Nick Oberlies, for being constant supporters of the book and in each of our lives.

Credits

Photo Credits

Thanks to John Boyer (Johnston Mill Nature Preserve), Allison Greiner (Linville Gorge and Elk Knob State Park), Calissa Holder (Greensboro Downtown Greenway Freedom Cornerstone), Ted Partrick (Greensboro Downtown Greenway Tradition, Motion, and Innovation Cornerstones), Switzerland Cafe, and Famous Louise's Rock House Restaurant.

Other Credits

Maps throughout this book were created using ArcGIS® software by Esri. ArcGIS® and ArcMap™ are the intellectual property of Esri and are used herein under license. Copyright © Esri. All rights reserved. For more information about Esri® software, please visit esri.com. The Outdoor NC Leave No Trace Principles are copyrighted by the Leave No Trace organization. To learn more visit www.LNT.org. For information on how you can protect North Carolina's Outdoors visit www.OutdoorNC.com.

About the Authors

Palmer and Hollis met in Greensboro, North Carolina, when their daughters became best friends in elementary school. They have hiked and biked many miles together on trails and roads ever since, including a 50-mile backpacking trip on the Appalachian Trail, the 40-mile Bike New York, and RAGBRAI, the annual 500+ mile bike ride across Iowa. Hollis and Palmer love all kinds of trail adventures and never pass up the opportunity to fuel themselves with delicious (and mostly nutritious) eats.

Palmer McIntyre

Palmer began exploring trails with her family as a young girl, backpacking with her father and learning about wildflowers from her grandmother. Palmer has worked with Piedmont Land Conservancy since 1996, helping protect natural areas in the Triad region. In 2020, she helped launch and leads the NC Great Trails State Coalition, a statewide trails advocacy group. She served as director for 2023 NC Year of the Trail, a statewide campaign to celebrate trails. Palmer settled in her native Greensboro after years away for college and work, including two years as a Peace Corps Volunteer in West Africa. She holds a Masters of Regional Planning degree from UNC-Chapel Hill. Palmer and her husband have three children and love to spend time on her family's forever protected farm in Ashe County.

Hollis Oberlies

A runner all her life, Hollis usually sits still just long enough to pick a new route, tie up her shoes, and get back out there again. Her passion for adventures in nature, and a knack for finding the best foodie stops, fueled the idea for *Trails & Treats*. In her youth, food was always a focus with her family, exploring different local favorites and new flavors. Her move to North Carolina in the late '90s introduced her to the vast network of trails to explore, which she, her husband, and two children have been traversing ever since. Hollis lives in Greensboro, where she is owner/operator of a graphic design business, coaches a middle school cross country team, and directs races which raise funds for local causes. Hollis was the recipient of the 2019 Will Caviness Award, given to one runner each year in memory of the Greensboro firefighter and runner. This book is, in part, a legacy of that award.